NOMADIC ARCHITECTURE EXHIBITION DESIGN BY EDGAR REINHARD

NOMADIC ARCHITECTURE

HUMAN PRACTICALITY SERVES HUMAN EMOTION

EXHIBITION DESIGN BY EDGAR REINHARD

TEXT BY ADALBERT LOCHER

LARS MÜLLER PUBLISHERS

Reinhard's work is remarkable: powerful, memorable and imaginative.

But perhaps the most extraordinary thing about the man is that he is still toweringly successful at a time when some marketing and communications people might feel that there is no need for his kind of work at all. After all, who needs trade fairs and exhibitions when the Internet and other technological marvels can bring everything into your home and office?

OK, we all know the answer to that: there is no substitute for personal relationships, meeting people, face-to-face discussions, eye contact and all that.

But, the argument runs, you can have all these things without paying a fortune for what are likely to be, however beautiful and full of impact, ephemeral pieces of three-dimensional design and construction. And anyway, what about cost effectiveness? How many people visit a show compared with the numbers of people who visit a corporate web site? And what is the relative cost of each visit?

I have to say that this 'rationalist' argument collapses when being fair about the context of the best trade shows and faced with the reality of Reinhard's spectacular and magical work.
Yet, even if you brush these points aside, there is the second line of argument. Where does the trade show fit into the new holistic approach to corporate communications? And more particularly, where does Reinhard's work fit?

The new thinking, to which the world's most sophisticated corporations now subscribe, is that the advertising campaign, the new product launch, the web site, the Chairman's speech, the internal communications video and all the rest of it contribute to, and are part of, an integrated programme of marketing and corporate communications.

Surely, within this context, the grand set-piece show stand cannot be an integral part of a corporate whole. Although it may have a secondary role in bringing people together, in a world of co-ordination, integrated marketing and communications, it must surely be a costly irrelevance.

In the hands of designers of lesser calibre, this might be so, but this is where Reinhard's skill, perhaps amounting to genius, emerges. At his best (as he so often is) Reinhard manages to capture the spirit of the client and encapsulate it in his design work. His exhibition design for trade fairs projects a three-dimensional version of corporate identity.

So, I believe that perhaps the most remarkable characteristic of Reinhard's quite extraordinary achievement is that, at a time of the most dramatic and turbulent changes in communication and marketing techniques and tools that I can remember, he manages to keep his work relevant, powerful and at the heart of his clients' mind set.

And this of course is not only a tribute to the work of Reinhard, but to the wisdom of his clients.

Wally Olins, London

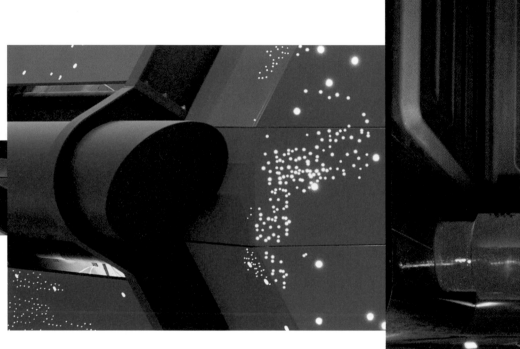

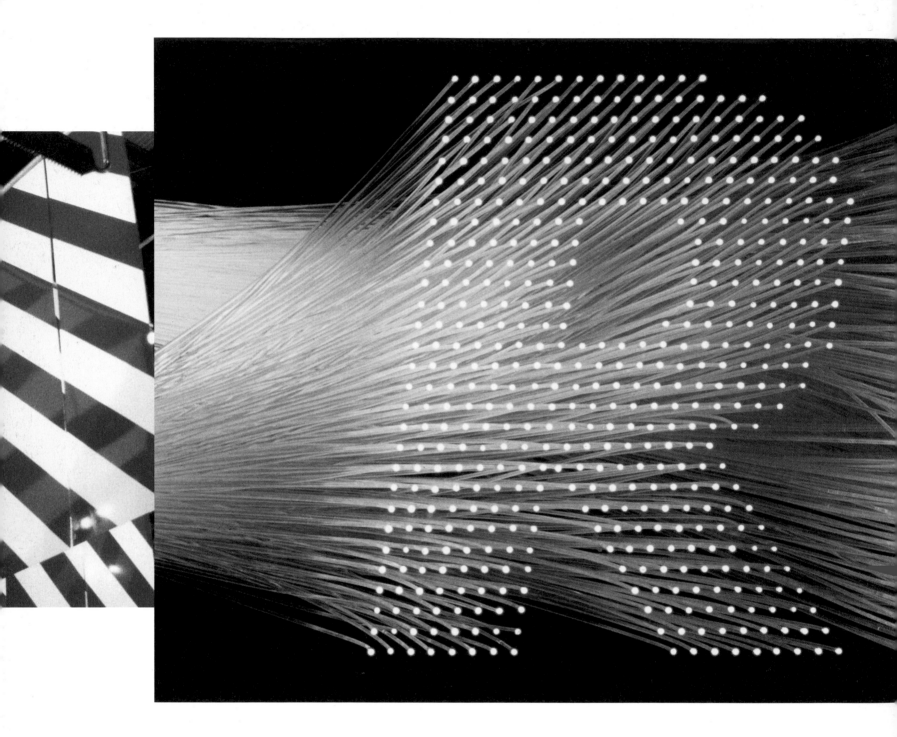

The

Tent

The scene has been a familiar one through history: people wandering from place to place, from country to country, offering their wares for sale. Their market stalls, indeed their homes, go with them. They can be put up quickly, and quickly taken down again.

Does this still happen today? Not quite. Now goods and people wander from continent to continent. Market halls are being pulled down in European city centres, and in the outskirts we build the desert wastes that we call exhibition centres – hall after hall for trade fairs, linked up with airports and motorways: *faits accomplis* of town planning and functional architecture. Then inside the hall we have the hubbub of the market, a partly fascinating, partly repellent mêlée of people, goods and offers, a chaotic mixture of smells and sounds, colours and shapes

The ancient high cultures grew up in the great river valleys of the Near East. The transport arteries brought people together, and they exchanged their products with each other. Tiny Neolithic market hamlets grew into trading cities. A temple was built on the ziggurat, a high, stepped tower, in honour of the town's god. Prosperity and religion started to overlap.

Thousands of years later the first world fair took place: London's Great Exhibition of 1851. Large exhibitions had been organized, usually by individual countries, in the 18th and earlier 19th centuries, primarily to present industrial products and thus also to promote and fix the national identity by showing scientific, technical and industrial achievements. But it was not until the Great Exhibition in the Crystal Palace, which was on a global scale, that new standards were set for future industrial exhibitions by the focal points it established: industrial products, mechanical engineering, raw materials, fine arts.[1]

Gradually trade fair cities were established; they made a world-wide impact, and pointed the way forward. In 1889 Alexandre Gustave Eiffel built his steel monument for the Paris World Fair; in Germany, Frankfurt, Hanover and Berlin became trade fair metropolises. World Fairs took place all over the world in the 1960s and 70s – in Seattle, New York, Montreal, Osaka. In the 1990s a gigantic trade fair site is being conjured out of thin air in Leipzig. At home and abroad cities are fighting over which is the best venue for trade fairs. Even smaller cities are making enormous efforts not to be sidelined.

For example, the diplomatic city of Geneva has just pipped Berlin to the post for the leading telecommunications show Telecom, which will take place on the Rhone again in 1999 for the sixth time in succession, thanks to investment in infrastructure and the headquarters of the Union Internationale de Télecommunication. This show has grown to such an extent that charter flights have to be organized all over Europe to cover the lack of hotel beds in the Geneva region. But site advantages of this kind, which can be said to have been inherited, are the exception and not the rule. And there comes a point when cultural facilities, a beautiful setting and a good reputation are no help at all if other venues are offering rock-bottom prices. Whether the various competing cities are not tearing themselves to pieces in this way is another question altogether.

Catch-as-catch-can in the hall
Outside, the competition between venues is raging, but in the halls it is the exhibitors who are trying to outshine each other. First of all, sheer size seems to have become the only yardstick – the firm who has the largest stand, rising as high as possible into the roof of the hall, has already scored a lot of points at the leading shows. The materials are also important – for a time, marble, steel and glass were indispensable if you wanted to make an impression. And finally there is the design. It is certainly not the uppermost consideration in the trade fair business. In all these hectares of occupied space, it is in fact relatively rare to find a presentation that has not just been thrown together and decorated using standard parts – one that can show a coherent concept covering all the spheres involved: corporate identity, corporate design, marketing, product design. Trade magazines then talk about 'designer stands', as if some of the stands had not been designed at all. 'Product' is deliberately placed last on this list of factors affecting a trade fair stand. In a world where products are

scarcely any different in terms of price and function, distinctions can scarcely be made simply through the products themselves.

The communication aspect is getting more and more important.
The production of goods and thus the world of trade shows have moved into a new phase in the developed countries. Just as communication is being increasingly taken over by the media, where mobile phones and the Internet are replacing personal meetings, the communication aspect of highly developed products is becoming increasingly important. Their qualities are no longer immediately evident to the eye, but hidden in the potential of the built-in electronics, which are not immediately apparent to the customer. Services and long-term qualities like adaptability to new technologies are product advantages that have to be communicated. Here the trade show as a medium benefits from the traditional advantages of direct confrontation and ambience. Wouldn't anyone who has the choice rather buy fish from the fish market with all its gossip, aromas and flirtation than from the deep-freeze cabinet in the supermarket next door?

Often this market character is given a boost at trade shows by means of spectacles of all kinds – sometimes more than is useful. The result is a setting that can become as essential as the set in a theatre. A set in a theatre is genuine, and there are good ones and bad ones. But trade fairs are not theatre, even though they have tended in that direction recently, and this approach is now taken for granted in the worst cases. Unlike the theatre, a trade fair is not offering just illusion, interpretation of the world and perhaps some spirit too, but the fair is itself a piece of the world (something that could be said about the theatre as well, but let's leave it at that). Fairs are about money, about products, about firms who are responsible for jobs, about shareholders' interests, about success and turnover, about unambiguous information, about the reliability of a relationship between partners. Here showiness is suspicious at first. A trade fair stand's quality as an event cannot derive from something copied. The stand itself is the event; it is not permitted to be anything else and must not want to be anything else.

Limited ability to plan

Of course people try to grasp feeling and emotion via intellect, in a cloudy edifice of psychological and marketing vocabulary. From time to time there may be some necessary arguments here, which have become unavoidable in the decision-making labyrinth of large companies, where an idea has to be placed above all hierarchical structures. Hence there is something erratic about a successful trade fair stand. It is ultimately not possible to predict whether a concept will actually take off, whether all the planning efforts will ultimately have the desired effect on the public, and so it can scarcely be planned down to the last detail. I am thinking of stands in which every detail is right, which are carefully designed in terms of material and construction, and yet leave me cold. A successful stand must have that essential quality that is more than a sum of its parts.

There is no other way of explaining the success of a 'one-off' like Edgar Reinhard. He has a degree of intuition that is scarcely definable as a recipe for success, and that is also difficult to convey. It was no coincidence that the Museum of Modern Art put its artistic reputation behind a retrospective of the work of Lilly Reich, a great designer of stands for trade fairs, in 1996. Outstanding trade fair design is tied up with individuals who point forward in new directions. For example, the installation Reich created using earthenware for the 'Deutsches Volk – deutsche Arbeit' (German people – German work) exhibition in Berlin in 1934, in its essence still sets a standard today. We cannot talk about direct influence – posterity was not reminded of Lilly Reich's work again until the MoMA exhibition in 1996 – but the two designers' work nevertheless has a great deal in common. They both see their work as architecture to some extent, without giving priority to that aspect. They are economical in their use of words, they allow the exhibits to speak by skilful arrangement, reducing visual signs to the core of the intended message. They successfully synthesize two- and three-dimensional resources. Admittedly these have become infinitely more powerful since Reich's day. This means that the need for reduction and selection is all the greater.

Specific architecture

Architecture, interior design and product design are synthesized in trade fair stands. It is not a matter of actual architecture, or of design. It is an independent discipline. Certainly major architects have sometimes been involved in exhibition design recently, including Santiago Callatrava and Jean Nouvel. It is not difficult to see how the architecture of the stand takes priority for these architects. This does no service to the matter in hand. A stand that is an architectural manifesto has failed. The criteria are different from those of architecture. Alfred Janser wrote of 'ephemeral small architecture in diffuse surroundings' in an architectural magazine.[2] He said that the independent nature of 'stand design' had never been in dispute and had repeatedly contributed to a general discussion on architecture. However, Reinhard's 'architecture' always has a quality of its own. His 1971 inflatable cathedral for Dow Chemical is not architecture, even if he is playing with an architectural form in the broadest sense. The same is true of the floating pavilion in prefabricated steel for IBM in 1987, 91 and 95. Just as nomadic peoples developed their own kind of accommodation, a trade fair stand needs its own particular qualities. And here again this is not very different from architecture. Log cabins for example, a common temporary architecture, were an early form of system building and often dismantled, transported and rebuilt in a new district that could be a considerable distance away – also after some years if not decades. Conversely, conventional steel construction or other forms of prefabricated building are used for large trade fair stands. The two disciplines have most in common when they fail – that is, when they turn out to be a mere backdrop.

Despite the considerable expense that is associated with trade fairs, the job of building for them is as good as non-existent in the public consciousness and as far as training is concerned. The special nature of the job has not yet been sufficiently accepted. So why should we be surprised that overall design concepts tend to be an exception?

1 Matilda McQuaid, *Lilly Reich and the Art of Exhibition Design,*
   Museum of Modem Art, New York, 1996.
2 Alfred Janser,'Ephemere Kleinarchitektur in diffuser Umgebung', in: *archithese* 3/96.

How does a chemical company provide information about water purification products?

Dow Chemical Europe
IFAT, Munich 1971

This inflatable, transparent hall has an ecclesiastical feeling to it. It is a plastic cathedral. And its elemental feel suited one of the four elements being represented here: water.

Dow Chemical used this stand to advertise its water purification products. No one can miss the point: visitors to the arched hall walked on plastic cushions filled with water and, as a promotional gift, they were given water in a plastic cube.

It is always difficult to show the effect and quality of chemicals – in this instance it is about the purity of water, which is so easy to destroy. This fragility is indicated by the almost immaterial hall construction. The visitor did not need consciously to perceive this symbolism. The crucial factor is the emotional contact when walking on the wobbly packs of water. This is a sensual experience – involving the eye, the sense of touch and the sense of balance.

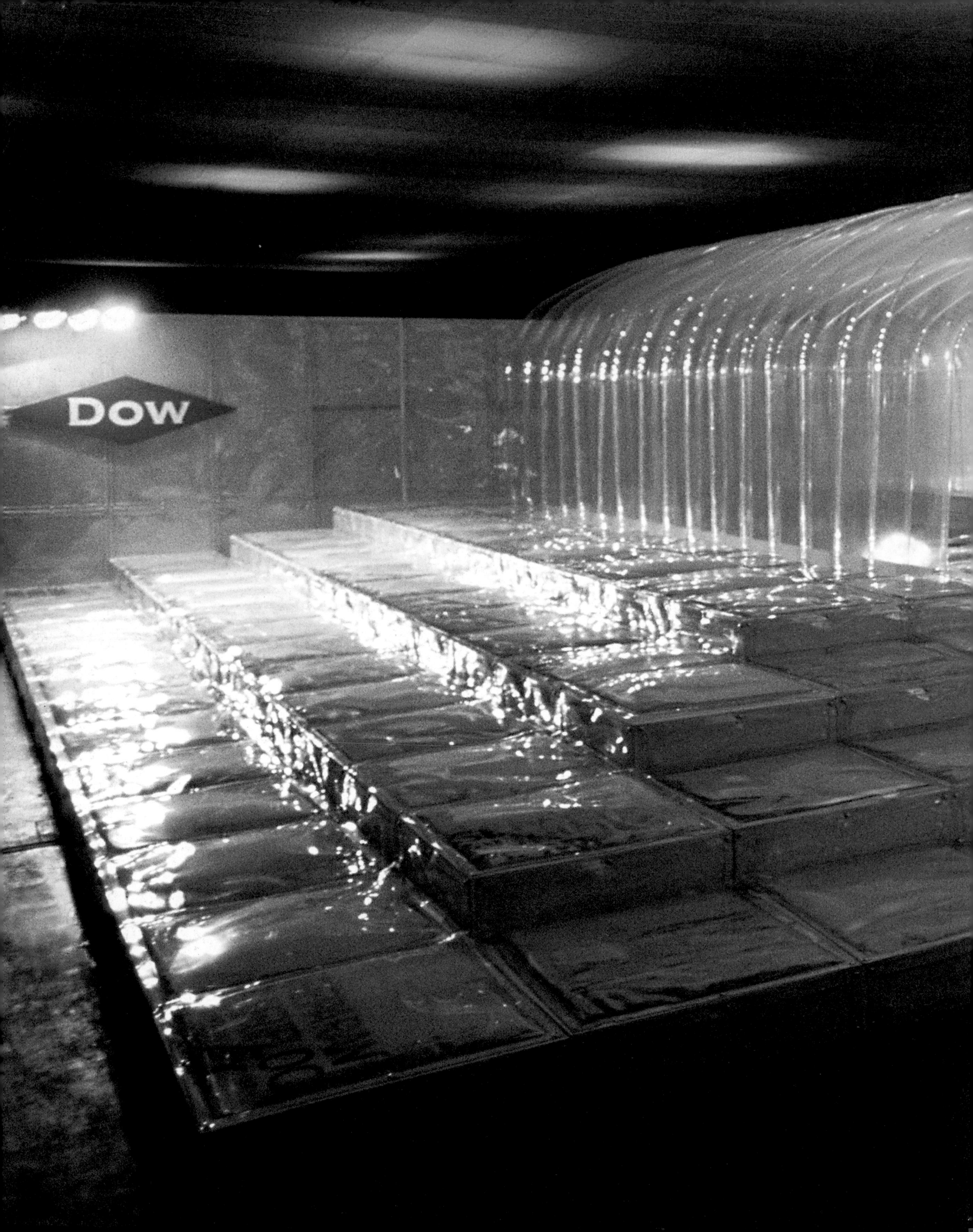
DOW

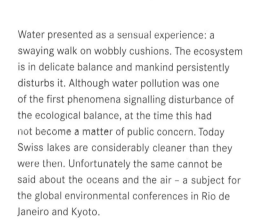

Water presented as a sensual experience: a swaying walk on wobbly cushions. The ecosystem is in delicate balance and mankind persistently disturbs it. Although water pollution was one of the first phenomena signalling disturbance of the ecological balance, at the time this had not become a matter of public concern. Today Swiss lakes are considerably cleaner than they were then. Unfortunately the same cannot be said about the oceans and the air – a subject for the global environmental conferences in Rio de Janeiro and Kyoto.

The unusual structure has its perverse side. The night before the exhibition opened, the plastic hoses burst as the heating came on in the hall. When the design engineers arrived in the morning, a few hours before the first visitors were expected, they found a crumpled heap on the floor. It was too late to repair the burst seams, so the plastic cathedral had to be permanently inflated and kept in shape by compressors for the duration of the exhibition.

side view

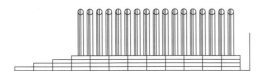

section

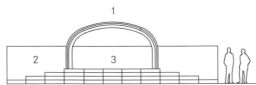

floor plan

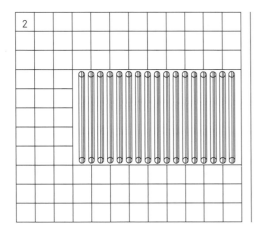

scale 1:300

1 Inflatable, transparent hoses with pressure
   compensation valves.
2 Water-filled plastic cushions that can be
   walked on.
3 Conference area.

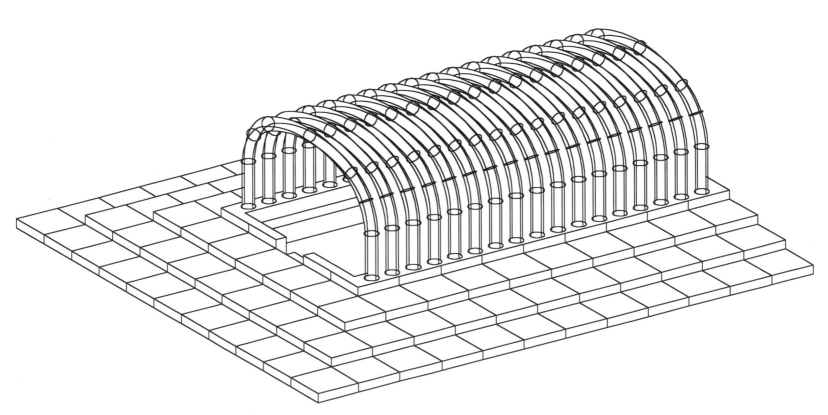

From products to solutions.

IBM
World Exhibition of Telecommunications
Geneva 1987

IBM used this stand three times for its presence at Telecom in Geneva, the world's most important telecommunications show. State delegations make decisions about telecommunications systems for their countries at Telecom, and contracts worth millions are agreed. The show took place for the first time in 1983 and reflected the enormous pace of development in this sector.

After his successful show in 1983 (page 227) Reinhard won the commission for 1987 after a competition presentation (page 283). The show was to be even more impressive than the previous one.

A container 350 square metres in size floated five metres above the hall floor, supported by four corner piers. People circulated freely on the ground floor. The 'spaceship' was entered in the middle via a flight of steps (later a lift), rather like an aircraft. The association with a spaceship was perceived as a message about IBM's know-how, and responded to the advertising slogans 'Solutions for a small planet' and 'Communications for the global village'. The building of stands is also a matter of logistics. The 200 tons of steel were erected by six men in about ten days. The four columns (1987 version) needed 60 tons of concrete, and the eight ground anchors for the piers (1991 and 1995 versions) were let into foundations 17 metres deep. The ground area was 850 square metres. About a month was needed for the technical installation of hundreds of kilometres of cable and countless pieces of equipment. Twenty-five lorries were loaded and scheduled so that the materials could be assembled directly from them.

Between the three shows, the large components were stored in the open air, and they were sand-blasted and primed before being used again. The structure was demolished in five days, the interior equipment in ten.

Edgar Reinhard operated for IBM as a sole trader, which meant that as the person responsible for building he could have been subject to liquidated damages in the event of failure. The steel construction company involved (Schneider Jona) had a considerable share in the success of the project.

1

2

1 All the supplementary equipment such as modems, distributors etc. are accommodated invisibly in the containers.
2 Red, system-like cable distributors symbolize interlinking.
3 The pavilion is clearly zoned: clients are briefed on the first floor before being taken down to the presentation area below.
4 The steel structure rests unfixed on the support of the piers. They are constructed like bridge bearers to take up expansion and contraction.

3

4

1 Prefabricated hollow concrete elements,
  bipartite, for use as the infrastructure.
2 Stay pipe, diameter 100 cm, tripartite,
  wall thickness 10 mm.
3 IPE 600.
4 Conference area with variable spatial divisions
  for four to 120 people.
5 Three-part staircase.

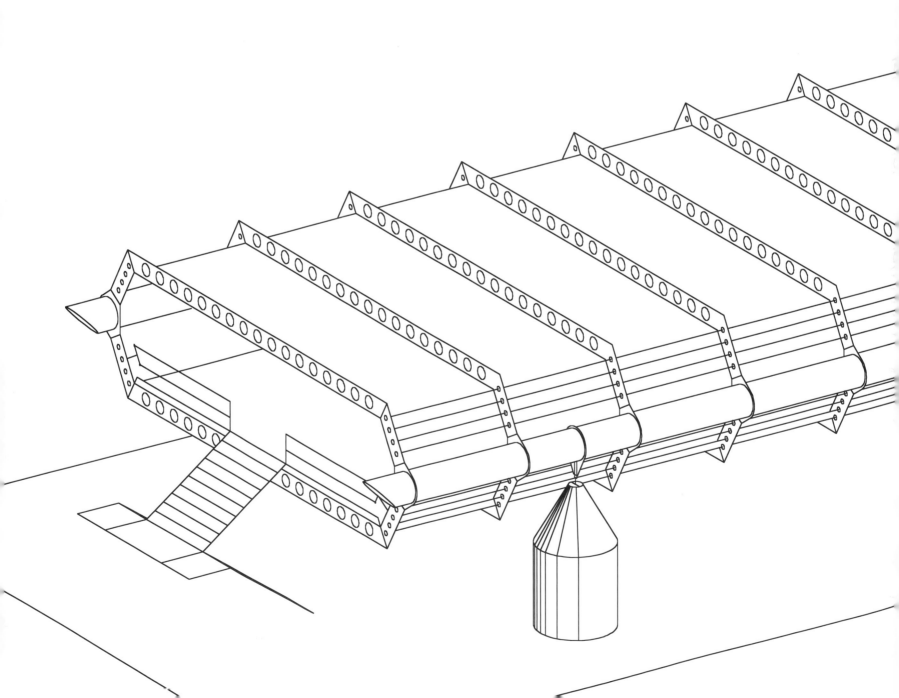

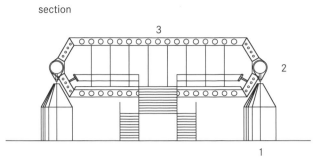

3

2

1

side view

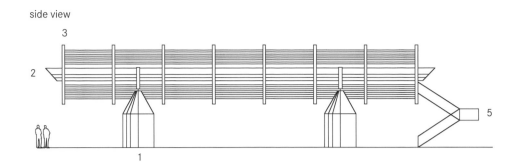

3

2

1

5

floor plan

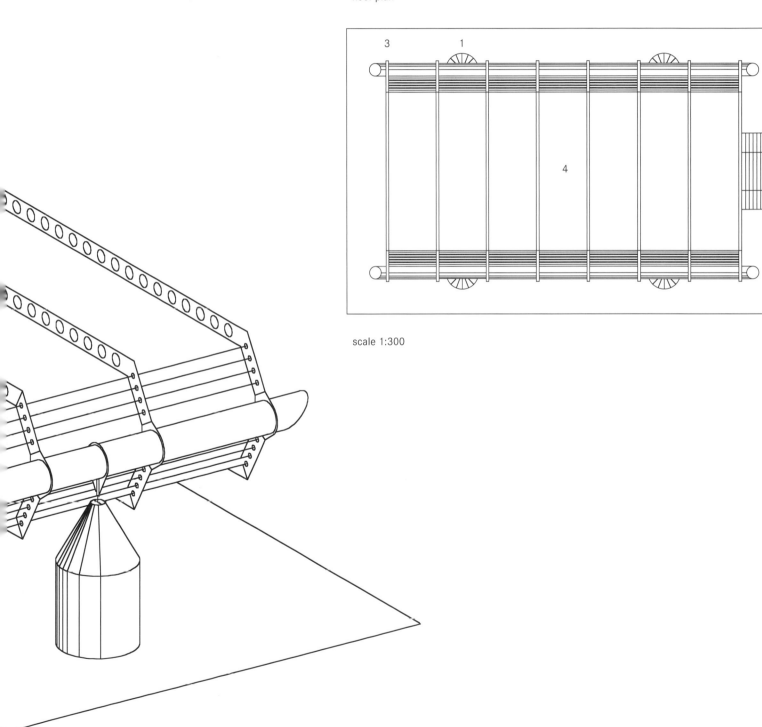

3   1

4

5

scale 1:300

Assembly 1987

Assembly 1991

The weight and length of the individual parts
conform to European standards in such a way
that they can be transported without police
escort. The parts are lifted by crane directly
from the lorry into the building site – a masterly
logistical achievement by steel contractor
Schneider of Jona (Switzerland).

Let the visitor do something and he'll take a good look.

Silent Gliss

Heimtextil, Frankfurt 1994

Subsequently used several times a year.

This producer of high-quality curtain rails and slatted blinds had to make a mark in an extremely homogeneous market. Instead of showing the products up front, Reinhard hid them away. They were enclosed in containers two metres above floor level, open at the bottom and fitted with curtains. When the visitor touched a button, a curtain was lowered and the rail tried out.

A striking, free-standing communication point in the form of a circular counter formed a contrast with the freely disposed containers, where things could be tried out unhindered by sales staff. The counter tower accommodated storage space and a refrigerator for hospitality.

The stand could be set up in a very short time by the company itself and fitted out with new samples each time. The containers were lifted by a fork-lift truck and the legs screwed on. Cabling for lights and motors were built in and only needed to be connected up. For reasons of cost, iron was used for the containers and left in its natural state. The rust on the surface, which was consciously taken into account, was used to contrast with the high-tech elements.

1

1 The containers are equipped by Silent Gliss themselves. The firm's own staff can even do the fit-up. The meeting counter is always in the middle.

2 Lighting for the bar counter.

3 The container is lifted on to the supports by the fork-lift truck.

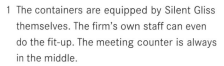

floor plan

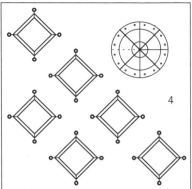

4

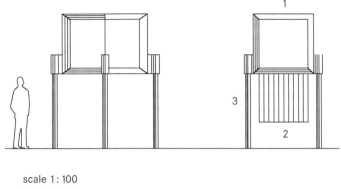

scale 1 : 100

variation

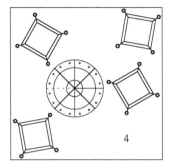

4

scale 1 : 200

1 Reinforced steel container, with integral
   screw-on low voltage halogen system.
   Linear motors for exhibit panels.
2 Clients can pull out the required exhibits from
   the service unit.
3 During the fit-up the container is raised by
   fork-lift truck so that the supports can be
   inserted.
4 No conventional stand structure is prescribed.
   Thus the container locations can adapt to any
   requirement.

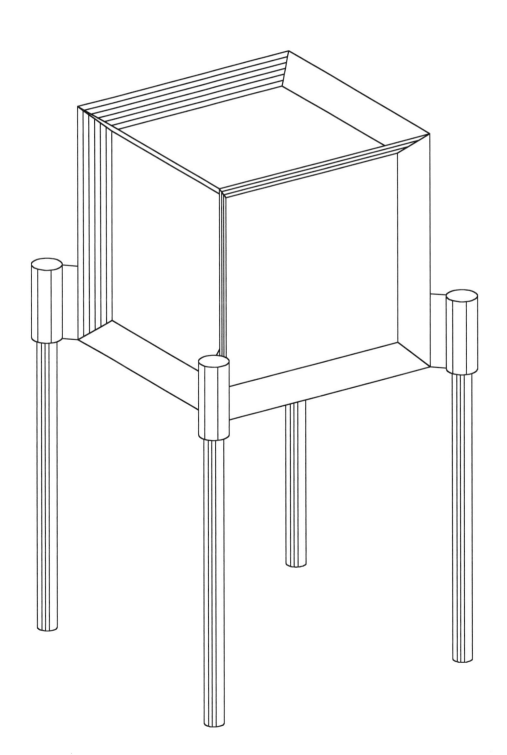

Also think of the people who have to build your stand.

Dow Chemical Europe
Modular construction system for
conference rooms. 1970s

Deep-drawn aluminium panels can be assembled as shells with very little effort. The walls are so light that they can easily be carried around by one person.
These shells were used on a number of occasions, for example at presentations by Dow Chemical.
Beads are pressed into the sheets so that thin sheet aluminium can be used. The deformation guarantees the stability of the surfaces. The material for each base container is transported in a folding crate. This means that less storage space is needed for empties.

1

modules in various sizes

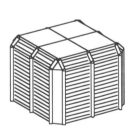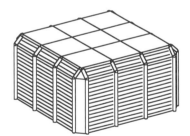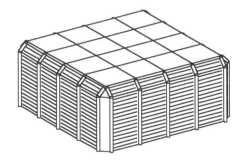

front view   adjustable heights for various exhibition halls

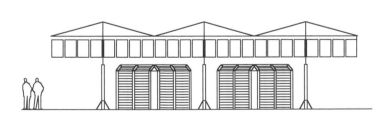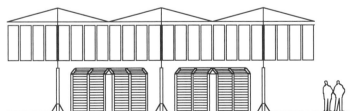

scale 1 : 300

1 An intelligent system saves fit-up expenses:
  it is quick, and needs little manpower.
2 Dow Chemical Europe, Sitev Geneva,
  Automotive Supply Industry Show
3 Dow Chemical Europe, Interplas Birmingham

2   3

It must be possible to put the tent up and take it down quickly.

IBM Germany
Travelling exhibition system
Project study 1988

This exhibition concept was intended to replace an exhibition train. Such trains are usually parked in unattractive areas in goods stations. Tent modules made it possible to exhibit in areas near the centre. A requirement was to be able to move between two locations within 24 hours, and special assembly cranes were developed for this purpose. Circus-like construction was planned for a fit-up time of 24 hours per unit.

The weatherproof units were intended for cities where there are no suitable trade fair halls, especially in former East Germany. Containers are arranged rectangularly and the tarpaulin is set up above the inner courtyard. The bearer supports are integrated in the containers, which are already cabled and equipped with computers so that the network can be up and running within a few hours.

The basic module for this series tent is a 12 metre shell. The roofing can be put up in a very short time using a fabric structure.

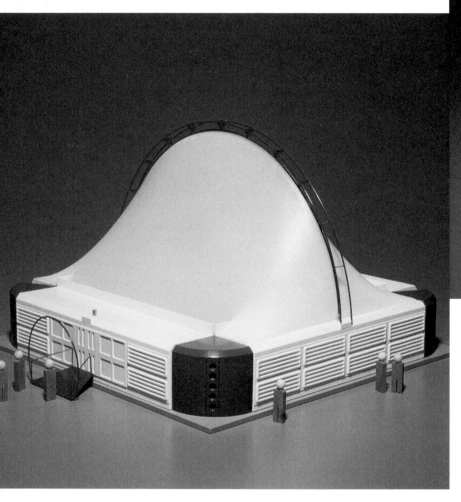

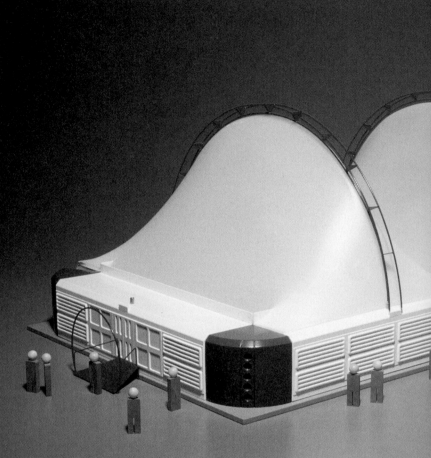

1 The textile membrane can be folded up
  like a pram hood.
2 The corner segments contain the technical
  installations.
3 A basic unit consists of four containers that
  can each be extended by two more.

front view

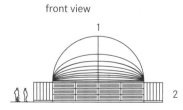

scale 1:400

side view

single module

module in series

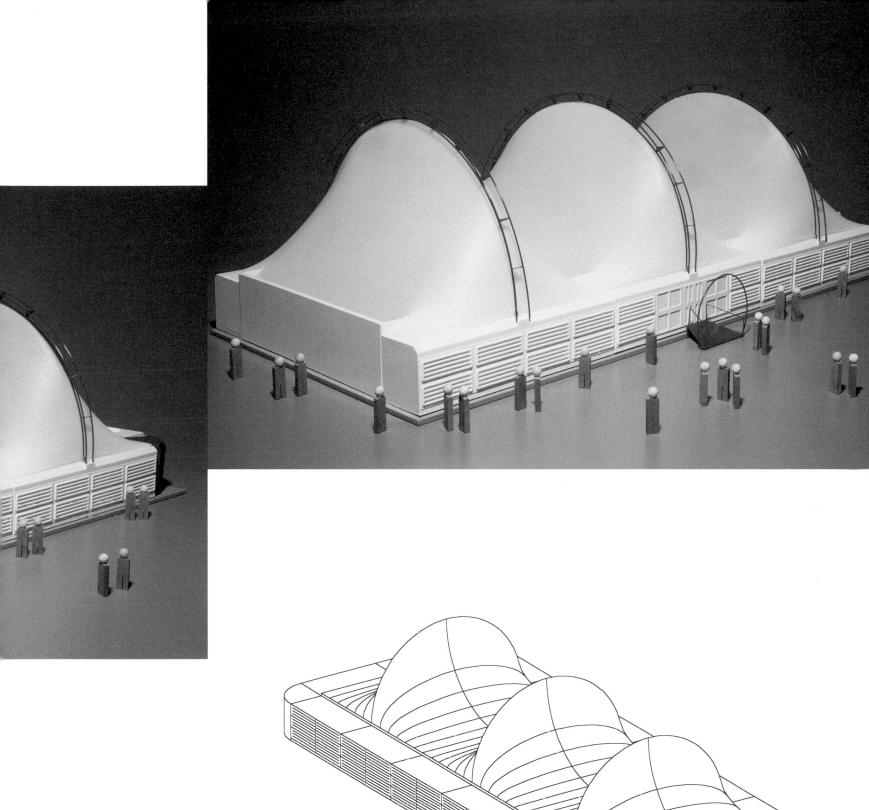

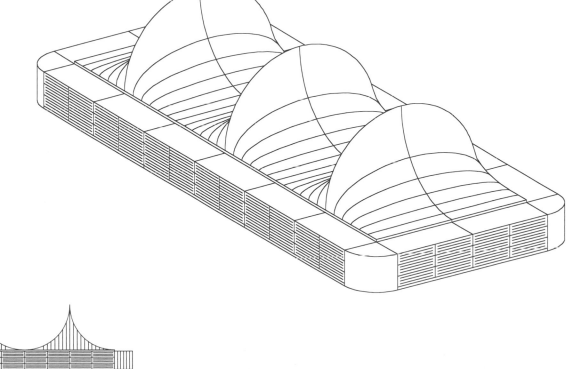

Messages

& Signs

Every stand at a trade fair is transmitter and receiver at the same time. The stand designer determines what it transmits. And the stand designer can at least influence what it receives. A stand is not a static manifesto, but a changeable podium that is not the same thing at the end of a show as it was at the beginning. Neither is a stand a general store that can accommodate the client's every wish. A good stand can do a lot, but not everything.

Hartmut Ginnow-Merkert analyses the product-person-product relationship using 10 information channels:

1. The product's visual transmitter
2. The product's visual receiver
3. The product's sound transmitter
4. The product's sound receiver
5. The product's tactile transmitter
6. The product's tactile receiver
7. The product's smell transmitter
8. The product's smell receiver
9. The product's taste transmitter
10. The product's taste receiver[1]

The remarkable feature of this design theory, of which only the chapter headings are given here, is the assumption that communication between person and product is reciprocal; from product to person and from person to product. Ginnow-Merkert calls the point of intersection the 'human interface'. As he says, the human interface 'conveys communication between person and product like an interpreter, it makes the product's statements to the person and the person's statements to the product comprehensible'. It is not difficult to establish that contemporary industrial products can address only a small part of human sensual potential and are even less tuned to converse reception. Even an apple can address more of our senses that most industrial products, however stuffed full of electronics they may be. And of course: an electronics giant made the apple into its company name and symbol. A brilliant move, embracing paradise and the moment of enjoying the fruit, and transferring these ideas to cool, technological products. But they do not turn into apples. Let us now extend these ideas to designing stands for trade fairs, and consider a stand as a product.

We can multiply the number of channels mentioned above immediately, because the stand as a product is not just the exhibit – whether it be an industrial product or a service – but a multiple of it. A stand is the intersection point of overlapping bundles of factors like, for example, the 'language' of the exhibiting company (corporate identity – CI), and the companies possibilities for visual expression (corporate design – CD). CI includes elements such as the company's communication patterns, in marketing, for example, or in the services offered, which again affect CD. Other factors are the specific nature of the show, its visitors, the other exhibitors, the technical requirements, deadlines and so on and so forth. This list is enough to show that a systematic method for mastering all the influential factors by analysis and thus synthesizing a stand must ultimately lead to paralysis. 'And thus the native hue of resolution is sicklied o'er with the pale cast of thought' – this line from Shakespeare's *Hamlet* should be taken to heart by anyone who sees an overall concept as an accumulation of everything needed. Clients are inclined to cram everything they can think of into a stand, seduced by the belief that this will mean that they do justice to everyone and everything. The opposite is true, and stand designers would do well to point this out to their clients.

The art of leaving things out

The art of building for trade fairs is the art of leaving things out. The reduction to a few signs is conspicuous in the hurly-burly of the show and will stick in the memory. It is all about abstraction of the main ideas of a company, about translating them into signs of all kinds that overwhelm the visitor's selection mechanisms and finally penetrate the deeper reaches of perception. Inexperienced visitors to trade fairs protect themselves from the flood of signals at the show by looking for detail and starting to rummage around. They are inclined to push aside information that in another context they would accept without further ado. The stand builder's usual reaction is to confront this defensive attitude by beating the drum even harder, straining for effect with 'eye-catchers', large letters, hordes of monitors and all the other aids available. This can mean that some visitors flee from the scene. Practice is a long way from design consensus among exhibitors. A sensible design code would turn a visit to a fair into a comprehensive experience.

A box of delights, then mutual stabbing to death

One popular piece of helplessness in this department is attempting to transplant a piece of so-called real life into the hall by the trick of a piece of scene-shifting. Experienced visitors to trade fairs, wholesale buyers, say, or someone responsible for technology in a company, are pleased to accept amenities but do not like being dazzled with trivialities. The people who stay are passers-by at the fair who really are looking for an experience or end-consumers who can still be outwitted if need be.

The charlatanism of experience will disappear from the halls as quickly as the charlatanism of design has given way to looking at things in a rather more substantial way. Which does not mean that nothing is experienced when the idea for a stand is good. But there is a difference between experience and trickery.

The magic word 'communication'

'Communication' is the most popular catchword for trade fairs, since mere product presentation went out of favour. As I suggested above, 'communication' can get out of control if it is not restricted and consciously focused. A stand requires 'unambiguous statements from pictorial language, textual information, stand architecture, the visual media, and ideas. It is only then that they arouse emotions, admit fantasies, trigger associations, and remain in the memory'.[2]

Edgar Reinhard's stands have an intuitive sign quality, which is unobtrusive yet clear. Reinhard does not see the sign as an extra, but as an inherent message. The sum of the entire appearance, the concept from logo to technical construction, is the sign. It is a consistent compression of all of a company's qualities, sometimes focused on a special achievement, for example when Toyota used its engine technology as a structural element of the stand. An outsize valve tappet is more than the sum of its parts when used as a support for the stand. The same symbol, a tappet that is merely enlarged to serve as an exhibit or eye-catcher, would just be an isolated gag. In a stand for Krause in 1989 Reinhard designed the central column as the mechanism of a ring binder, and the 'inserted pages' as consultation counters. Logical reduction of and simultaneous attraction by the few elements selected is the hallmark of these works.

Interaction

As established at the beginning of this chapter, communication is reciprocal, and the fashionable word to describe this need for understanding is 'interaction'. Where this does not take place, we are dealing with forms like the sermon, indoctrination, orders. These forms are inappropriate where people who are used to using their heads and hands have to be addressed. The stand designer has to ask himself: 'What does the stand do with the public?', and even more: 'What does the public do with the stand?'.

Since the rise of interactive technologies, the largest clusters of people are to be seen at stands where there are electronic toys. That is not surprising. No one will want to be a mere listener, spectator or receiver of orders if he or she has an alternative. People with a remote control in their hand change television channels at will, and they do the same at a trade fair. Admittedly this also makes people go too far. Individual stands are conceived almost as playgrounds – which may be appropriate for an electronic entertainment firm. But is it right for a motor-car manufacturer's CI to conceive his stand as a ghost-train of events, with his visitors piloted from attraction to attraction? It will certainly attract attention, but where will this attention be directed? Games and fun are important aspects of life, but not the most essential factor when one is buying a new car from the top of the middle range. Market research has discovered that the average visitor to a trade fair is more intelligent than previously, and thus has more rigorous requirements in terms of presentation and information, problem-solving and environmental protection.[3]

Edgar Reinhard used an interactive approach from a very early stage. In 1974 he used the Informat, a small projector that made visitors stand very close if they were to see anything, rather than gigantic images. On Wild und Küpfer's stand (1994) the exhibits were hidden in drawers, and visitors could only find them by doing something about it themselves. The principle is varied in a number of ways – in the 'Peep-Show' for Zürcher Ziegeleien in 1995, and elsewhere. This is the opposite of the habit of presenting products as loudly and conspicuously as possible and thus inducing a defensive response.

Stand staff and visitors are actors
The more visitors feel themselves addressed in different ways, the more they can act in different ways, and thus ease their resistance to the onslaught of goods and impressions. Here transparency of intention is crucial. Modern consumers and professional buyers have a nose for manipulation, they are not going to be taken for a ride and sold down the river. A trade fair is not a light entertainment broadcast, but a stage play with parts that are played by professional actors in extreme cases. At IBM Telecom in 1995 actors were flown to Geneva from America to play the parts of staff on stands. Rieter, the Winterthur manufacturer of spinning systems, went almost as far in 1995 when they had their large stand for Itma in Milan set up in advance in Switzerland so that the staff could be trained by role-playing; Rieter then transported the 'stage' with its 'sets' and 'actors' to Italy. Clowns who tried to draw visitors into conversation were the dot on the i. The exhibits, high-quality textile processing machines, were not working. They were painted by artists, and auctioned at the show. Anyone who wanted to see the machines working was driven to a factory.

Efforts on this scale are not possible for every show and every product. And it is also true that the most beautiful visual concept will go wrong on any stand that does not provide enough space for people to meet. Images, words and sounds can be reproduced as well today as ever before. They can no longer be the main items at a trade fair. The advantage that trade fairs have over other media is that people, suppliers and customers, meet each other. Promoting this is the principal purpose of a trade fair stand.[4]

1 Hartmut Ginnow-Merkert, 'Beyond the visual; Die Kommunikation Produkt-Mensch-Produkt und der unsinnliche Designer', published in Form Diskurs 1/96, *Journal of Design and Design Theory,* Verlag form, Frankfurt am Main

2, 3 Ingrid Wenz-Gahler, *Messestand-Design,* Verlagsanstalt Alexander Koch, Leinfelden-Echterdingen, 1995

4 Rieter's appearance at Itma 95 was based on an idea by Edgar Reinhard. The marketing department of Rieter Winterthur, the trade fair construction firm Alfred Messerli AG Wetzikon, the Design Team Aarau and Rigling/Bloch Konzepte Zurich were ultimately involved in it.

How can an advertising message be reduced to the core of the product?

K79 Plastics Fair
Düsseldorf 1979

Transparent strips of plastic with colourless granules welded into them hang from the hall ceiling like flags creating an iridescent labyrinthine effect and the illusion of a deep space. Plastic in granular form is inconspicuous – but as a material installation it refracts the light and seems like a valuable raw material.

Detailed information was provided on polyester columns by mini slide projections. Thus the spacious, grey-white environment makes an exciting contrast with the small-scale colour pictures, which have to be looked at close up. Visual 'micro-information' reaches its target audience, even amidst the flood of impressions that every exhibition has to offer these days if the design of the medium is to attract the necessary attention.

The concept evokes artistic installations and thus produces a high-quality identity for the company. In 1979, so-called 'culture' – seen as a manifestation of beautiful things – had scarcely been discovered as something that companies could borrow to enhance their image.

Dow was not showing cultural sponsorship, but company culture.

front view

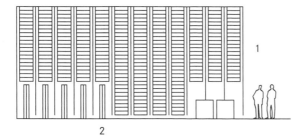

1

2

floor plan

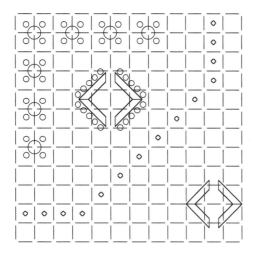

scale 1:200

Information columns with slide projections attract
attention from a distance. The slides show
possible uses for the granular material in the
transparent strips. The effect of the strips
is enhanced as the light changes.

1 One thousand metre-portion packs of plastic
  pellets were needed for this area.
  Other show appearances were designed to
  the same concept.
2 The information columns contain series of
  slides or 35 mm monitors.

78

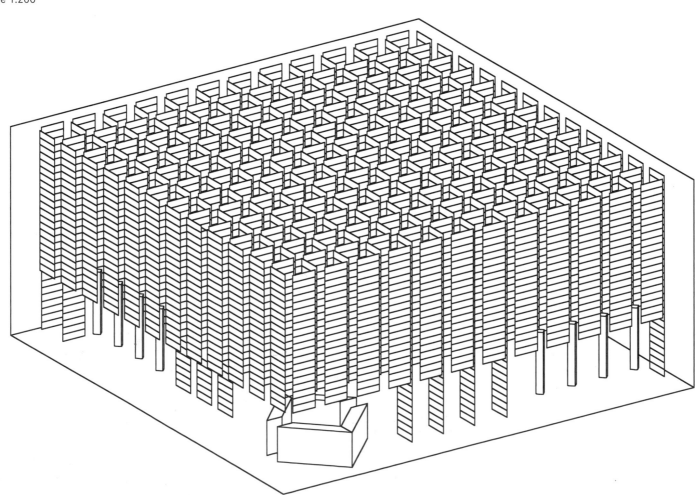

Let the managers grow wings.

IBM Europe
Paris 1984

From 1984, the board of IBM Europe always held their annual conference at this venue. The axially symmetrical arrangement with its stairs and various projection levels borrows from ecclesiastical and grand architecture. Axial steps have been abused in recent history but are still popular as a sign of prestige; it certainly pleased the managers and shareholders of this leading technological company.

Identical images were shown on the two projection areas in the foreground – they are, as it were, the wings of the eagle giving its report at the lectern in the centre. The screens can be removed quickly to give an unhindered view of film projections on the Cinerama wall. The concept has to meet requirements similar to those for a stage set, and the product or company presentations were designed with the assistance of artists.

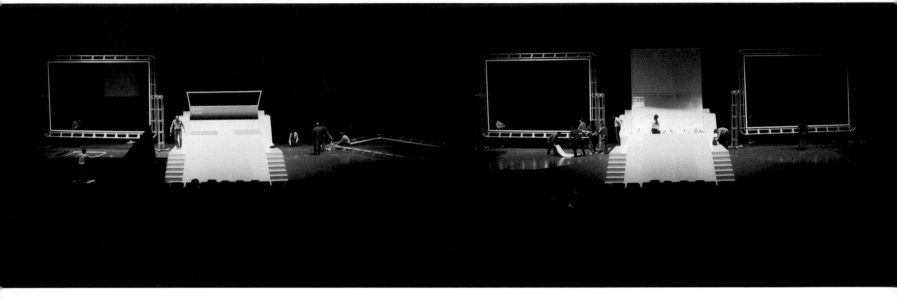

1 Lecture point with screen in position for
  speaker portrait.
2 Side screens moved away, central screen
  folded down: the Cinerama wall behind is
  revealed.

front view

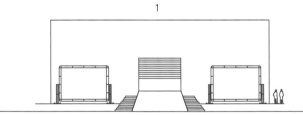

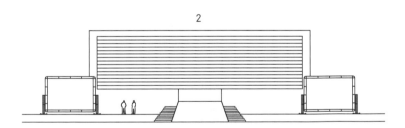

floor plan

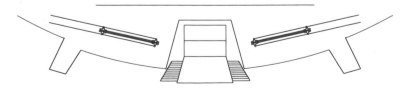

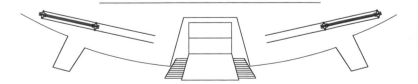

scale 1 : 500

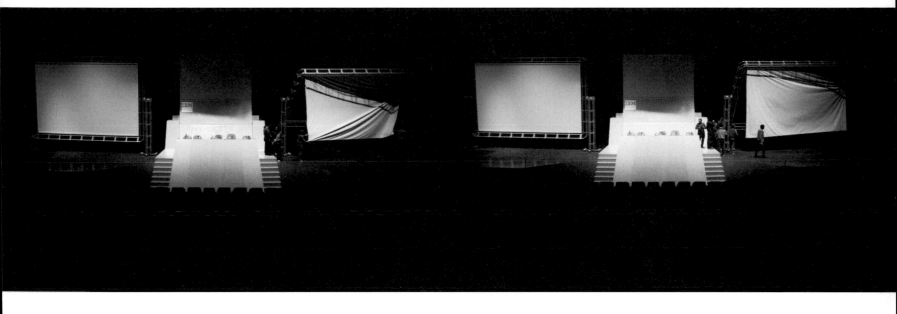

1

1 The side screens can be moved on rails. They
always show the same projection, so that
the audience has the best possible view on
each side. The central section can be opened
up for the large-scale projection by the person
at the lectern, and is reminiscent of a laptop.
There is a Cinerama screen behind the three
others, and when this comes into play the others
are moved away to the sides or folded down.
2 Synthesizer musician Bruno Spörri arranged
Antonio Vivaldi's classic *The Four Seasons*
in his own style. Expressive illustrations by
Willi Rieser were projected to accompany this
music. Arrangements of this kind provide
a captivating accompaniment to company
information.

2

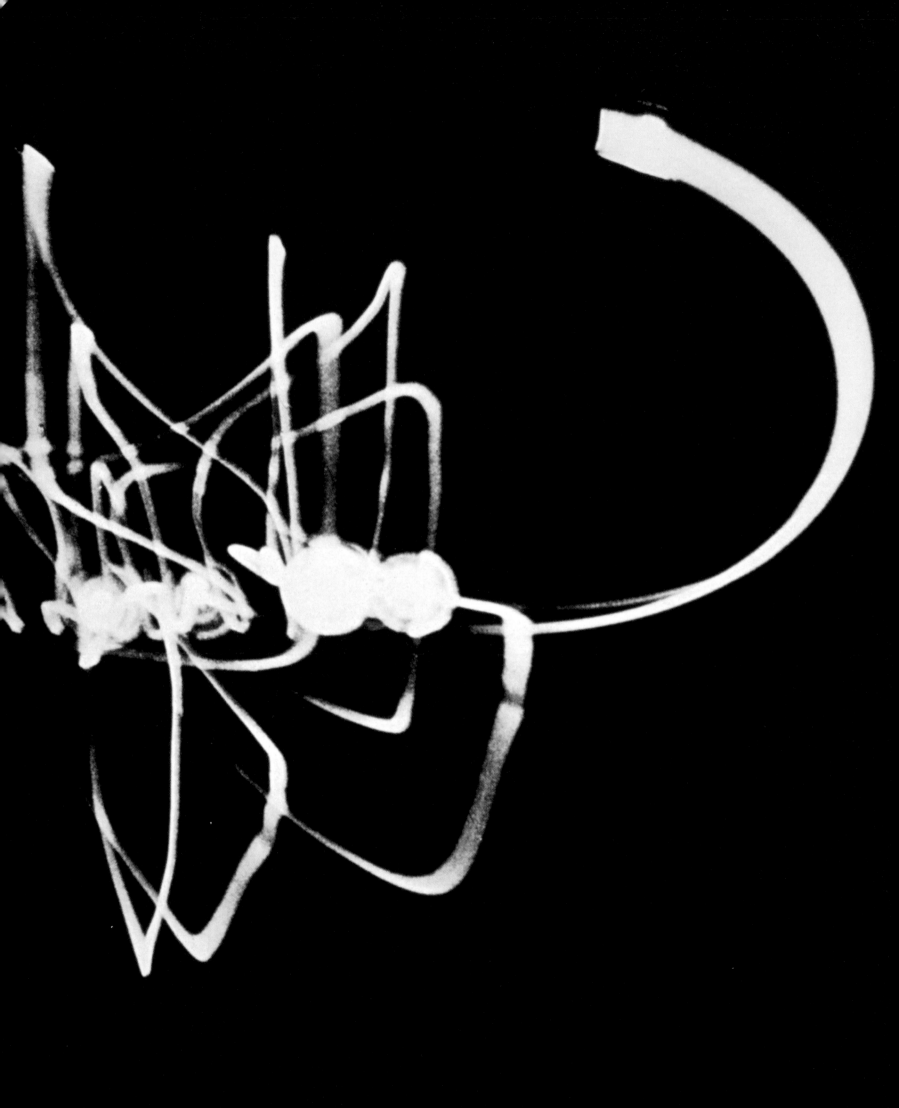

Reducing, enlarging, simplifying – effective signs can be created simply.

Little gifts foster friendships

Little mementos to give away to clients, technical tricks to demonstrate new achievements – the possibilities are endless. These examples shown go back to 1972 and demonstrate how tremendously fast visual presentation techniques have developed. The Informat looks astonishingly modern after almost 30 years. It was an apparatus for presenting slides with sound accompaniment – a primitive form of today's virtual reality masks. At that time IBM's 'golfball' typewriter was a supreme engineering achievement; it was followed by the 'daisywheel', and then the era of mechanical typewriters came to an end. As miniaturization progressed, the electronic revolution replaced even individual tools from scratch. And this created quite new problems for visual presentation: new symbolic worlds had to be invented for invisible mechanisms molecular in scale. The more trivial these worlds became, the more popular were the ever more complex systems. So, although nothing much has changed on the meta-plane of communication, things have tended to become more banal, which is something to which designers can also succumb: complexity has a banal face, simplicity has high-calibre tools at its disposal. A look at private Web sites on the Internet proves how true this is.

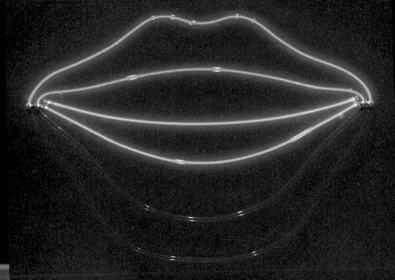

1

3

5

4

Ces photos illustrent la grande vitesse de composition de cette machine, qui ne dépend que de la rapidité de la dactylographe. La tête imprimante atteint une vitesse potentielle de 14 frappes à la seconde. Elle se remplace instantanément, d'un seul mouvement, 53 écritures faisant partie de 5 familles de caractères sont actuellement disponibles. Le texte de cette brochure a été composé par notre secrétaire, en caractères Press Roman demi-gras corps 11. Ce travail lui a demandé quinze minutes environ.

1 IBM Telecom
Chocolate keyboard

2 Dow Chemical Europe, IFAT Basel 1973
The problem of water pollution is symbolized by figures with coloured lights in random organic forms flowing ceaselessly over them. The fact that this apparently slightly threatening installation raised questions was precisely what was intended.

3 Dow Chemical Europe, IFAT Munich 1970
Water welded into plastic cubes.

4 IBM Dictation Equipment 1972
Display for IBM dictation equiment, where the neon 'lips' lighting up alternately suggest the movements of speech.

5 IBM Golfball
On the (light) track of new technology. The photographic hieroglyph shows the path followed by an IBM typewriter golfball when typing a line. The image was used for brochures and displays. Though rarely seen today, the golfball was the acme of typing technology at the time of 1965.

6 Informat 1974
  The Informat made its début in the Kunsthalle
  in Cologne as part of the 'Sehen und Hören –
  Design und Kommunikation' (Seeing and
  Hearing – Design and Communication) exhibition. The show attracted international attention, but was savaged by local critics – the
  technological promises it made probably came
  too early for most of them. The Informat
  shows sequences of colour slides in 3-D quality with stereo sound at stations with four
  peep-shows. These can be adjusted for height
  by the visitor. The 'spyhole' principle, which
  encourages people because it focuses their
  attention, appears in various forms in several
  of Reinhard's stand designs.

7 IBM Scanning Tunnel Electron Microscope   7
  It is enough simply to understand the principle.
  The window display enlarges the micro-
  dimension as a simplified macro presentation.
8 IBM Ink-Jet Window Display 1985
  Reduce it so far that everyone can understand
  it. The visual presentation of ink-jet printing
  technology for a window display uses an
  enlargement of the symbolically reduced
  technical process.

6   8

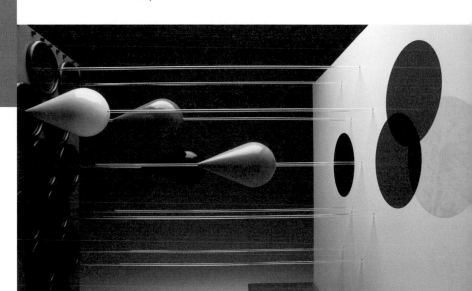

Hide the products so that they have to be discovered.

Wild und Küpfer
Swisstech, Basel 1994, 1996

The company makes injection moulded parts in plastic. It is difficult to recognize immediately the value of tiny precision parts; the visitor's interest has to be focused. Reinhard appeals to curiosity by literally hiding the parts. The visitor has to look for them, using a list of numbers, and find them in drawers. The spatial staging suggests the 'treasure hunt'.

The steel drawers are set between rough, archaic-looking granite wedges. The high value of nature and the durability of the stone are conveyed to the product.

The stand can be assembled by the client without expert help. The granite wedges are put in place by fork-lift trucks, the drawers inserted – and the treasure-chamber is practically ready.

This industry-support show was presented in highly technical surroundings. The emotional ambience was clearly distinct from this and guaranteed the stand plenty of visitors.

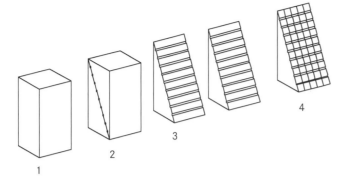

front view

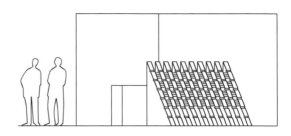

floor plan

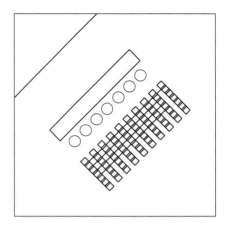

1:100

On the manufacture of the granite segments:

1 Rough-sawn block from the quarry.
2 Diagonal drill-holes as splitting holes.
3 Drill-holes and rough split surface head-on.
4 The halved blocks are sawn into slices.

The stone segments were hewn from a single
block. They can be positioned by two people.

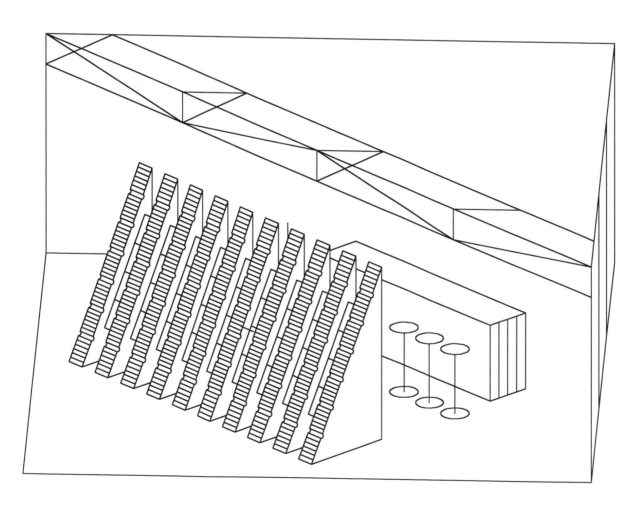

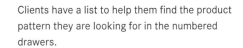

Clients have a list to help them find the product pattern they are looking for in the numbered drawers.

Hide the product.

ZZ, Zürcher Ziegeleien
Swissbau, Basel 1991

The vault, made of porous concrete bricks, is supported by a steel framework – in fact only half an arch, as the span is completed optically by a mirror. The complete product range is 'hidden' in chests of drawers with narrow glass fronts – a variation on the game described in the previous example.

The problem is how can a product be presented without it being submerged in the competing battle of products? The paradoxical answer is to hide it. This reticent product presentation makes the length of the contact area all the more important. The zones with the various communication patterns – introverted, extroverted, neutral – are clearly recognizable and help visitors to get their bearings and agreeably provide varying degrees of intensity.

front view

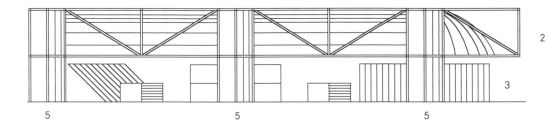

5   5   5

section

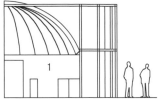

2

1

floor plan

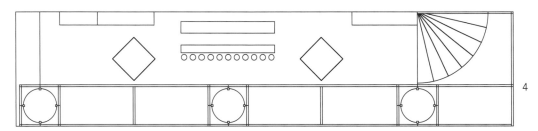

4

scale 1:200

1 Porous concrete brick vault.
2 Mirror surfaces double the half vault to make
    a full round.
3 Exhibition cases with perforated metal fronts.
4 The steel framework supports the vault.
5 Existing columned halls are clad with
    lightweight concrete elements.

Zones with various communication patterns

The roofing-tile drawers are arranged on the
slant-like pitched roofs. An illuminated peephole
on the front invites visitors to open them.
The drawer principle means that a large number
of products can be presented in a relatively
small stand area.

The framework – as the stand ceiling – carries
a half-vault made of porous concrete blocks
from the exhibitor's range; a mirror doubles it
up as a barrel vault.

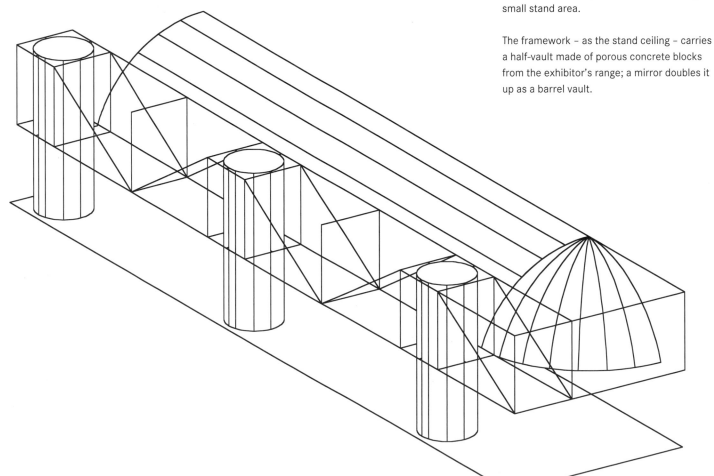

Keep objects of desire at a distance.

**ZZ, Zürcher Ziegeleien
Swissbau, Basel 1995**

By using the 'peepshow' concept, Reinhard pushes to the limits the principle of making a product inaccessible and thus all the more attractive. The visitor can peer at the product through windows in a dark container – in this way the product to some extent becomes an object of desire. The walkway enhances the effect of the staging – the curious visitor draws attention to himself, and thus becomes a protagonist. This concept proved difficult to grasp for some of the company's managers, but attracted higher than average attention from visitors as a topic of conversation.

For this stand, newly developed lightweight concrete elements were used for the façade structure. Thus the firm was able to launch a new product at the same time in the form of the stand construction material.

front view

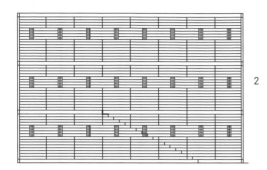

section

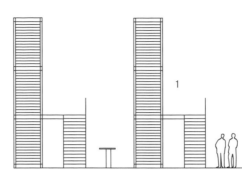

2

1

1 Steel skeleton as a support for the wall cladding.
2 Newly developed product (fibre cement slabs) used as stand construction material.
3 Columned halls determine the breadth of the two cubes.

floor plan

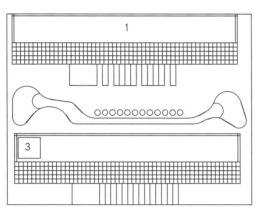

scale 1 : 200

A lot of people can make contacts in a short time at this bar without chairs or stools. The large areas at the end are intended for spreading out plans. There is a clear division between discussion and viewing areas.

Masonry details, façade sections, etc. are shown inside the cubes on a scale of 1:1.

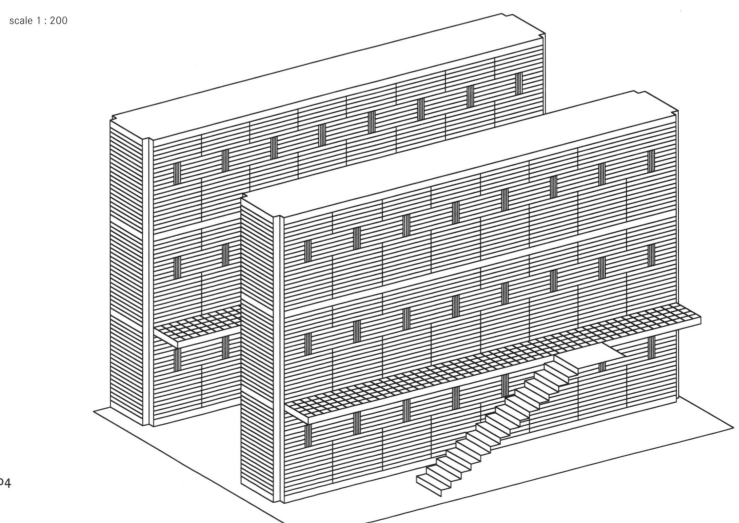

Corporate identity continued.

**NZZ, Neue Zürcher Zeitung
Basel 1992**

After several years with different stands, NZZ gave itself
a new platform in 1992 in the form of a series of reading
desks. Design elements are reminiscent of the forms in a
rotary press.
Realistic life-size figures arouse visitors' curiosity while
making the stand somewhat surreal. The well-tried quiz is
retained. The neutral, austere appearance is appropriate
to the image that the newspaper assumes with its conservative design and advertising campaigns.
A trade fair stand is part of corporate identity, not just a
detached spectacle.

section

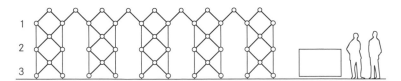

1 These tubes contain a low-voltage lighting plant.
2 Reading surfaces.
3 Foot supports.

floor plan

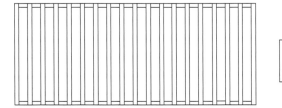

scale 1:150

Naturalistic dolls reduce the inhibition threshold in the apparently technical environment modelled on a rotary printing press.

This construction was redesigned every year in terms of colour.
First year: crude iron, galvanized sheets.
Second year: all white.
Third year: tubes blue, surfaces white (colours of the Zurich coat of arms).

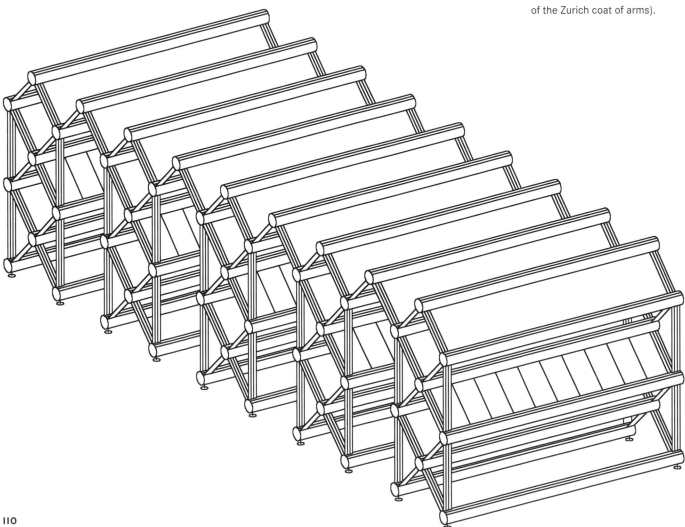

Time-travel for an industrial enterprise.

Sulzer
Science Centre, Winterthur 1984

The Winterthur diesel engine manufacturer has a distinguished heritage, and is now a high-tech concern. It presented its development as a journey though time, using a channel of historical settings.

A set designer built faithful copies of props and rooms from the firm's earlier days. Many employees came from families in the city and region of Winterthur, whose residents had been employed by Sulzer for generations. The exhibition brought periods to life that have definitely come to an end now that the firm has been restructured as a high-tech concern – a kind of farewell presentation.

1 All the structural elements, like wall panels and linking elements, are semi-finished products (galvanized sheets) used in ventilation technology.

2 Entrance and exit are reminiscent of suction heads, the ramp signifies the transition into another time.

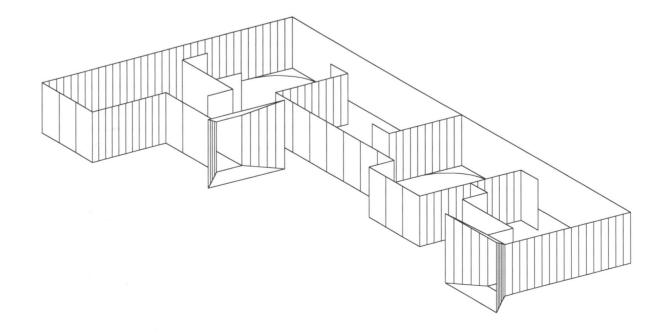

front view

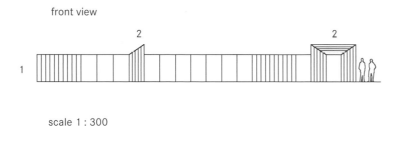

scale 1 : 300

floor plan

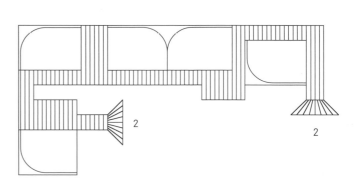

The entrance of the time-tunnel represents the
threshold to earlier times and the exit represents
the passage to the present day.

How do you turn a commodity into a brand?

Dow Chemical Europe
Dry Cleaning Show, Paris 1970

The problem: how do you turn a chemical cleaner, which is a commodity, into a brand? This was Edgar Reinhard's first stand project; it is already clear which way he is going. The exhibition stand consists of a labyrinth of barrels piled one on top of the other. It is a stage-set in the broadest sense, the visitors become protagonists and experience something. First comes the emotion, then the intellect. If the senses are affected, customers will warm to a product.

Use of the 'barrel' as raw material is so staged that it inclines towards the aesthetic. The trick of giving products an aesthetic quality by using a repetitive arrangement had been used by stand designer Lilly Reich as early as the 1930s (see introduction to Chapter One) and was also returned to later. Andy Warhol addressed the aesthetics of mass production with his screen prints like '200 Campbell's Soup' or 'Coca-Cola' in the 1960s. And later Christo, the wrapping artist, planned an installation in the form of a barrel pyramid. In Reinhard's case this use of the barrel installation for Dow Chemical again goes back into the product world itself – the product world absorbs its own artistic reaction with a flashback.

It is also not difficult to find artistic influences in Reinhard's later work. For example, the stone segments for the Wild und Küpfer stand in 1994 (page 90) where the segments were drilled and cut from the a single block using the same methods as the German sculptor Ulrich Rückriem (Essen). Or the plastic flags suspended from the ceiling for Dow Chemical in 1979 (page 75) which are reminiscent of the way that flags were used at the Swiss Expo 64 and in later artistic textile installations. Or the adaptation of large scale architectural forms like the triumphal arch for EniChem (page 121), religious forms (Dow Chemical page 31), temple allusions (IBM Europe Telecom 1983, page 227), and amphitheatres (Metallgesellschaft, page 259).

front view

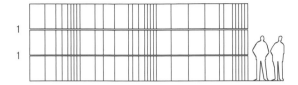

floor plan

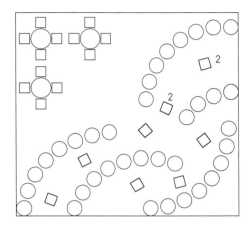

1 The barrels are screwed together
  by linking elements.
2 The sound of rolling barrels can
  be heard from the loudspeakers.

scale 1:150

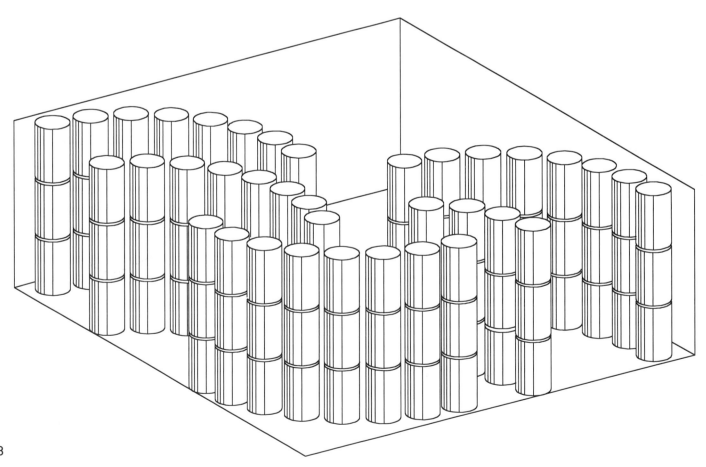

How can the exhibitor's national character be expressed?

EniChem
Plastics fair, Dusseldorf 1983

With his triumphal arch for EniChem at the plastics fair in Düsseldorf in 1983, Reinhard again turned to grandiose, historical forms, as he had with the plastic cathedral for Dow Chemical in the early 1970s. The group of three elements, placed in a row, was lit in the national colours red-white-green, thus giving the Italian state business a particular aura.

Anyone wishing to reach the products and range of services on the first floor had to go under the arch three times. In the old days going through an arch of this kind was a gesture of submission. This parallel was probably not intended, although the concern was presenting itself very powerfully here.

Polycarbonate double slabs, one of the exhibitor's products, were used for the arches.

A 20-second spot on the screens gave information about the product range. Visitors went under the arches to the reception area.

front view

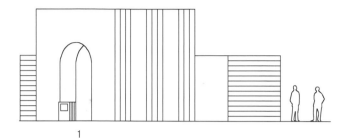

1 After the triumphant reception . . .
2 . . . a staircase . . .
3 . . . leads to the conference level.

1

floor plan

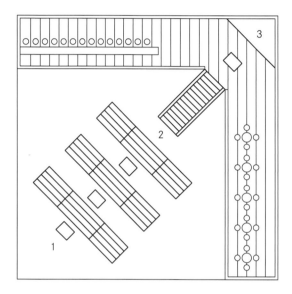

scale 1:200

Polycarbonate double slabs, one of the exhibitor's products, were used for the arches.

A 20-second video clip gave information about the product range on the screens. Visitors went under the arches to the reception area.

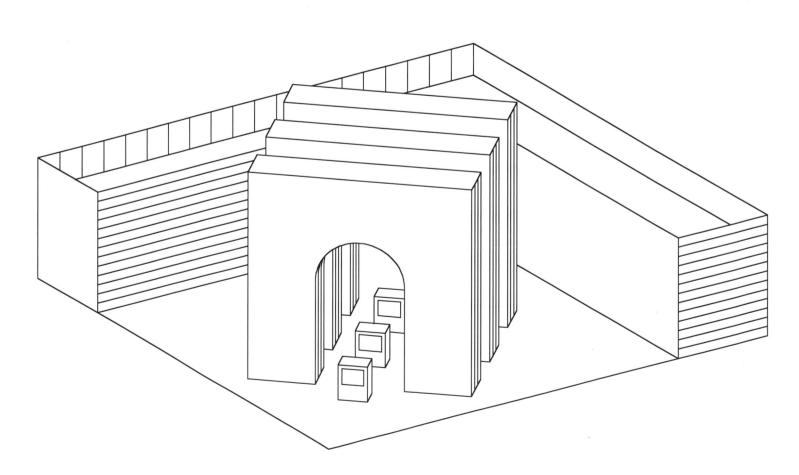

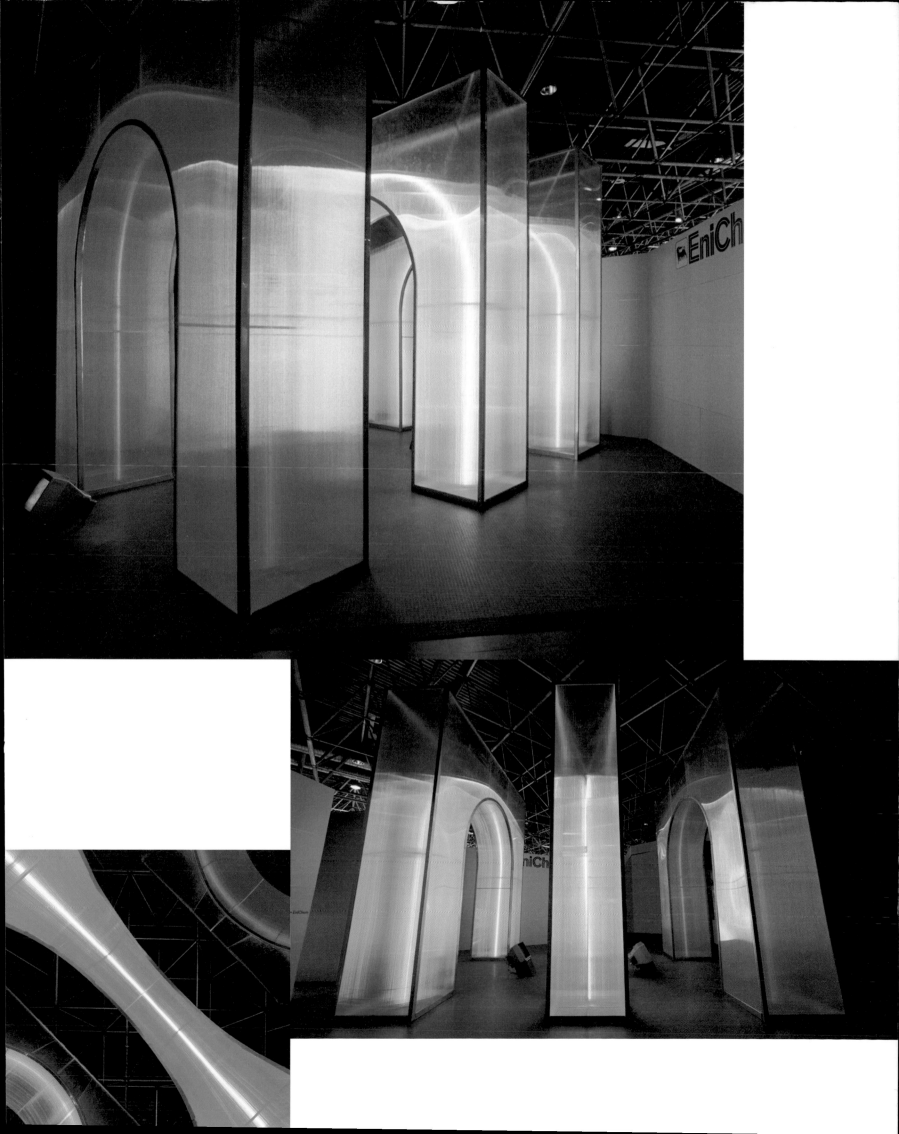

How does a leading car manufacturer tackle prejudice?

Toyota Tokyo
Geneva Motor Show 1990
Frankfurt, Paris, Birmingham, Brussels,
Amsterdam 1990–1998

At the time Toyota was the only car manufacturer to have introduced overhead twin-cam multi-valve technology for production cars. The stand was conceived as a sign of Toyota's advanced engine technology, consciously eschewing prestigious materials like marble and chrome that were fashionable with competitors.

The characteristic feature here is the way the stand's columns and supports are in the shape of outsize vertical tappets and horizontal shafts. Steel tubes one metre in diameter were used for this. The fact that the decorative signs – 'tappets' and 'camshaft' – are built into the structure makes them seem particularly credible, rather than just eye-catching elements added as an afterthought. Thus Toyota was able to communicate a promise of quality that was pitched very high, combating European consumer scepticism about Japanese car manufacturers.

Stand was used exclusively at European motor shows – in Frankfurt, Geneva, Brussels and Birmingham. It could be assembled lengthways in modules of one to four units. The basic framework could always be restocked, and floors could be built in as needed.

When submitting the project in 1989, Edgar Reinhard put forward the following considerations:
'BMW and Mercedes exhibition stands can hardly be beaten in terms of design perfection and execution. Visitors have grown accustomed to this "de-luxe" standard which uses stainless steel, granite, marble and extravagant audio-visual and display techniques – they hardly find it exceptional any more. One thing which is common to all Toyota cars and which is important to all Toyota clients is the favourable relationship between price and performance. This is of particular significance because Toyota customers represent a wide range of people with varying purchasing power and taste.'

'So, what can be done to draw attention to the corporate philosophy with the help of visual, architectural, design and construction engineering means? Toyota's leadership in technology must be reflected by the stand design. This approach will be more effective than the "me too" competition in the fashionable furnishing of the stands.'

Both the main piers and the junctions signify Toyota's progressive engine technology.
They consist of cast-iron sections, conventional steel structures and chromium steel for the supports.
The differing tolerances of these metal processes presented particular technical problems.

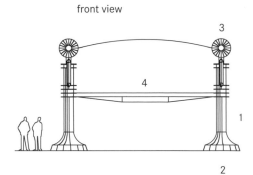

front view

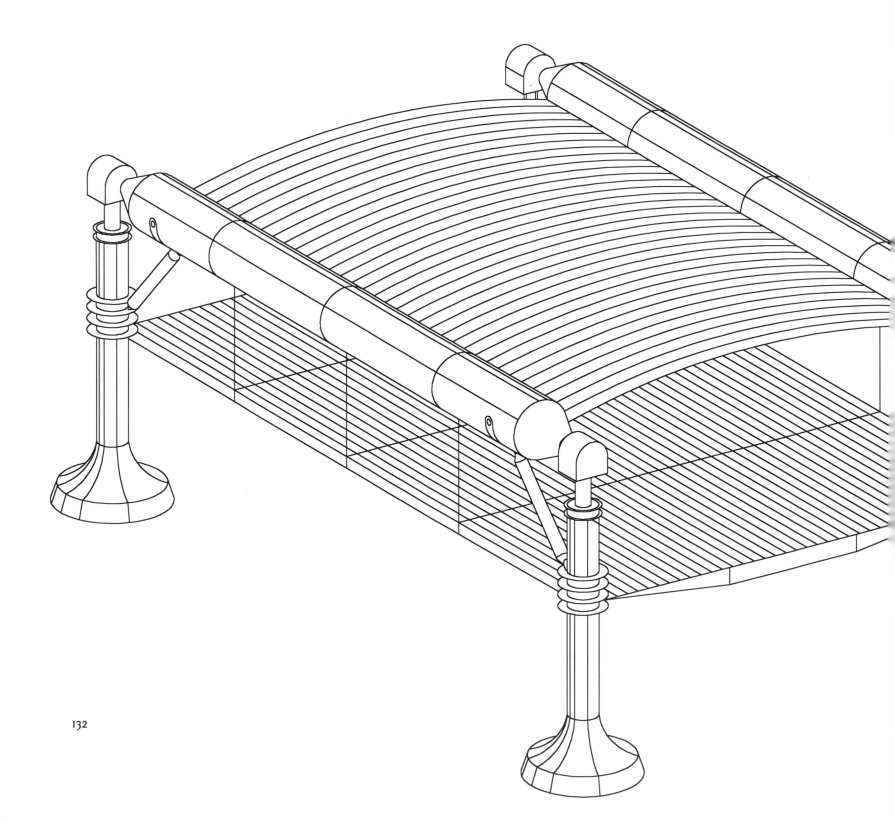

side view

3

4

1

2

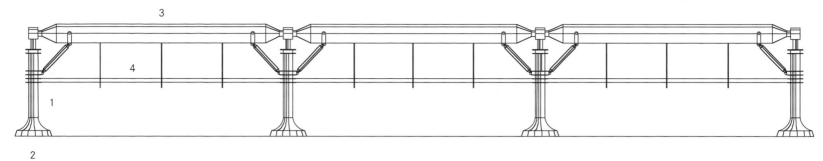

floor plan

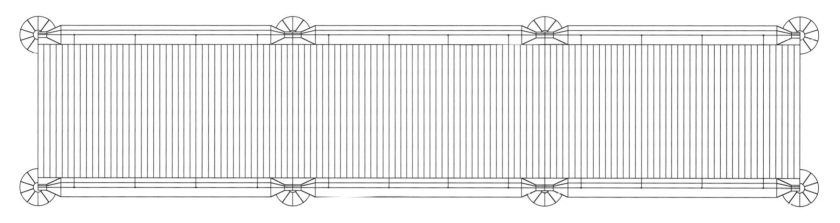

scale 1:200

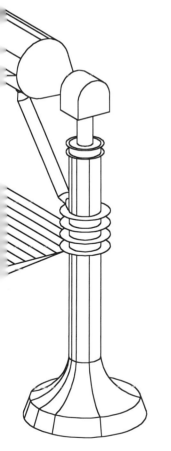

1 Valve guard. Steel tube with stainless-
  steel cladding.
2 Valve. Grey iron casting.
3 Overhead camshaft. Stay pipe 100 cm
  diameter.
4 Suspended conference platforms.
5 Layout with modules placed longitudinally.
6 Layout with modules placed transversely.

5

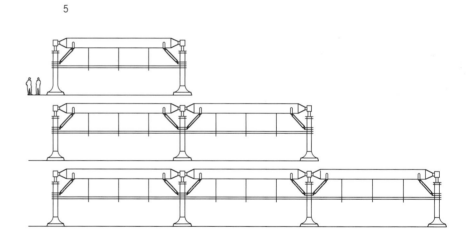

6

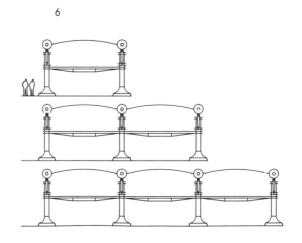

133

scale 1 : 400

How should the leader in an 'unfashionable' market be presented?

Krause
Plastics fair, Dusseldorf 1989

Seen in a different dimension, the 'ring binder', an unspectacular everyday object, becomes attractive in a quite new way. Here no additional décor is needed – the idea of designing the stand as an oversized ring binder in chromium steel speaks for itself and guarantees that the producer will be identified with his product. Krause is the quintessence of ring-binder mechanics, and this message sticks in the mind.

The 'leaves' of the ring book serve as a bar counter and information centre. This object was used for all shows as well as the in-house showroom.

Most of the stands at the plastics show are several hundred square metres in size. Although the stand was in a peripheral position on a upper floor, it was commended by an independent jury as one of the ten best stands.

front view

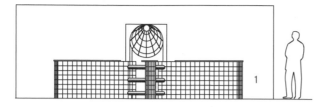

1

1 'Pages for notes': printed wooden counter.
2 Pull-out cabinet containing the full collection.
3 Glass counter.

floor plan

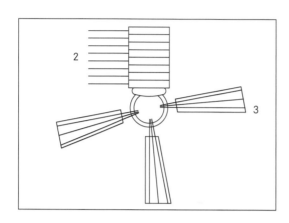

scale 1 : 100

Stainless steel, the original material, was used for the ring mechanism. The engraved Krause logo is also an enlarged version of the original.

The product range was presented in the background using pull-out cupboards. The counter was in the form of a file and was used as a product display in the firm's showrooms in between shows.

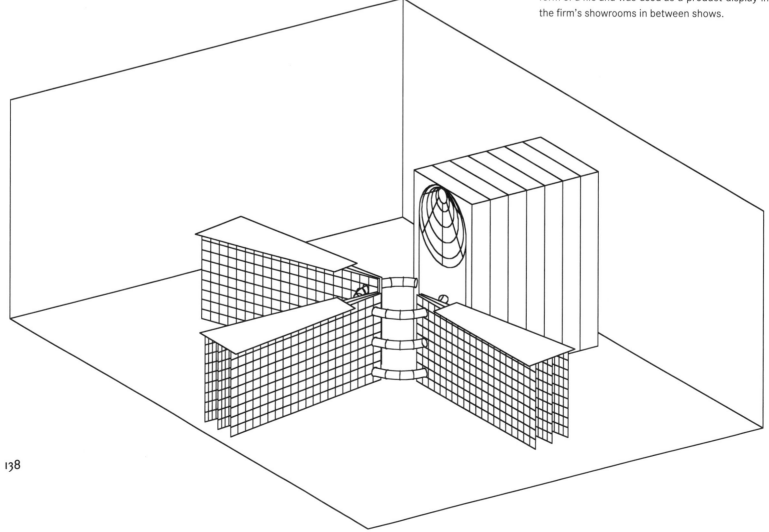

Making a direct connection between company name and product.

**Rieter Spinning Systems
Osaka, Greenville 1983, Paris 1987,
Hanover 1991**

The Winterthur textile machine concern, a leading company worldwide, used this stand for eight years from 1983, in venues including Osaka, Greenville, Hanover and Paris. The system structure permitted modular assembly covering l00 to 900 square metres in a very short time.
The fully air-conditioned, sound-proof pavilion was used mainly in hot, humid parts of the USA and Japan.
The company's technological competence is symbolized by its specially designed logo (by Wirz, Zurich). The fibre-optic strands of light evoke textile threads, in other words the product of Rieter's high-quality spinning machines.
It is traditional that major contracts in this branch of industry are always transacted at ITMA, the International Textiles Machine Show in Milan. Every piece of equipment is planned specifically for the client. For this reason it has to be possible to negotiate in a quiet atmosphere, without distraction.

Hanover 1991

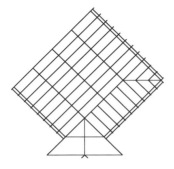

front view

floor plan

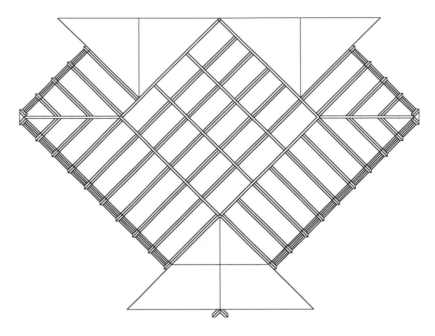

scale 1 : 400

Paris 1991

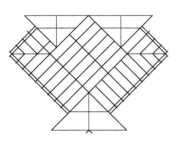

Osaka 1983

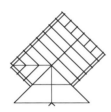

Scale 1:1000

The hermetically sealed meeting container was conceived for textile trade shows in humid, hot areas of Japan and the USA. It was fully air-conditioned – and soundproofed as a protection against noise from the machines that were being presented. The aluminium elements are constructed as noise protection panels.

Steel skeleton as substructure for the sound-absorbent element planking. The grid is laid out in such a way that it can be adapted to different stand areas.

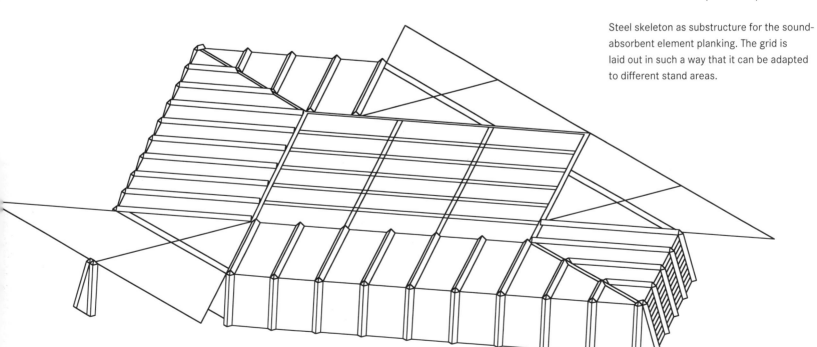

What does a manufacturer of building materials do when the market is depressed?

ZZ, Zürcher Ziegeleien
Swissbau, Basel 1993

The prefabricated concrete elements are supported on struts and carry pallets with stacks of bricks. But the great weight of the many tons of material is an illusion. Only the outer layer is real, the rest is a dummy. Lights and mirrors create a conducive atmosphere in the interior. This staging with its building-site look signals cost-conscious thinking – and yet the stand's plainness gives it an air of exclusivity. The display cabinets from the 1991 stand were reused, this time on the second floor.

After the building industry had been in decline for years, this stand presented a working building site again. The quasi-realistic impression is a clear sign of the key message: building with bricks. The meeting counter was deliberately planned for standing room only, to maintain a steady flow.

front view

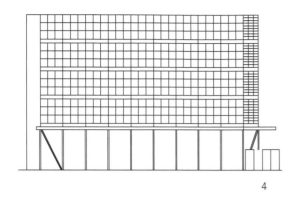

side view

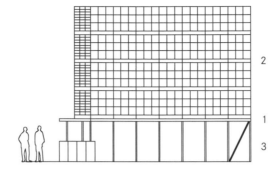

2

1

3

4

floor plan

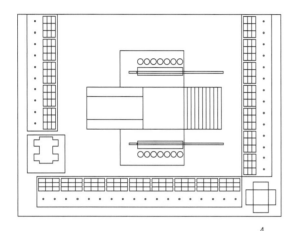

scale 1:200

4

1 Prefabricated concrete element.
2 Bricks on pallets, invisible polystyrene core.
3 Dimensioning the stays as inconcreting floors.
4 Reception.

The 1991 pull-out cupboards (page 94) were used again under the steps to the stack, parallel with the bar counter. The concrete support slabs were made by a subsidiary company of Zürcher Ziegeleien.

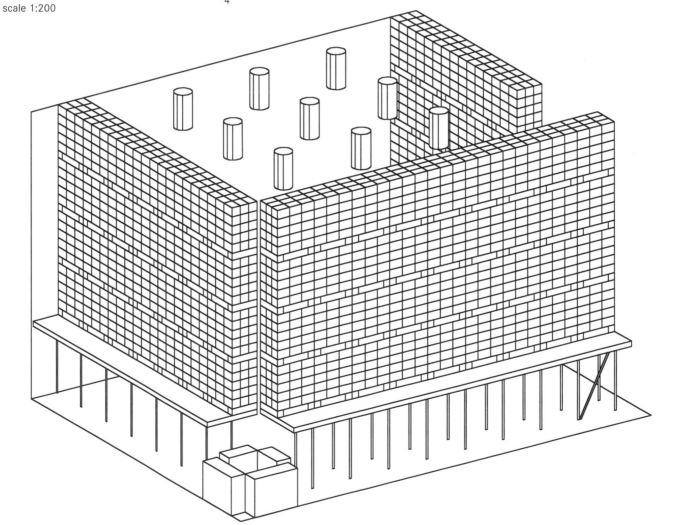

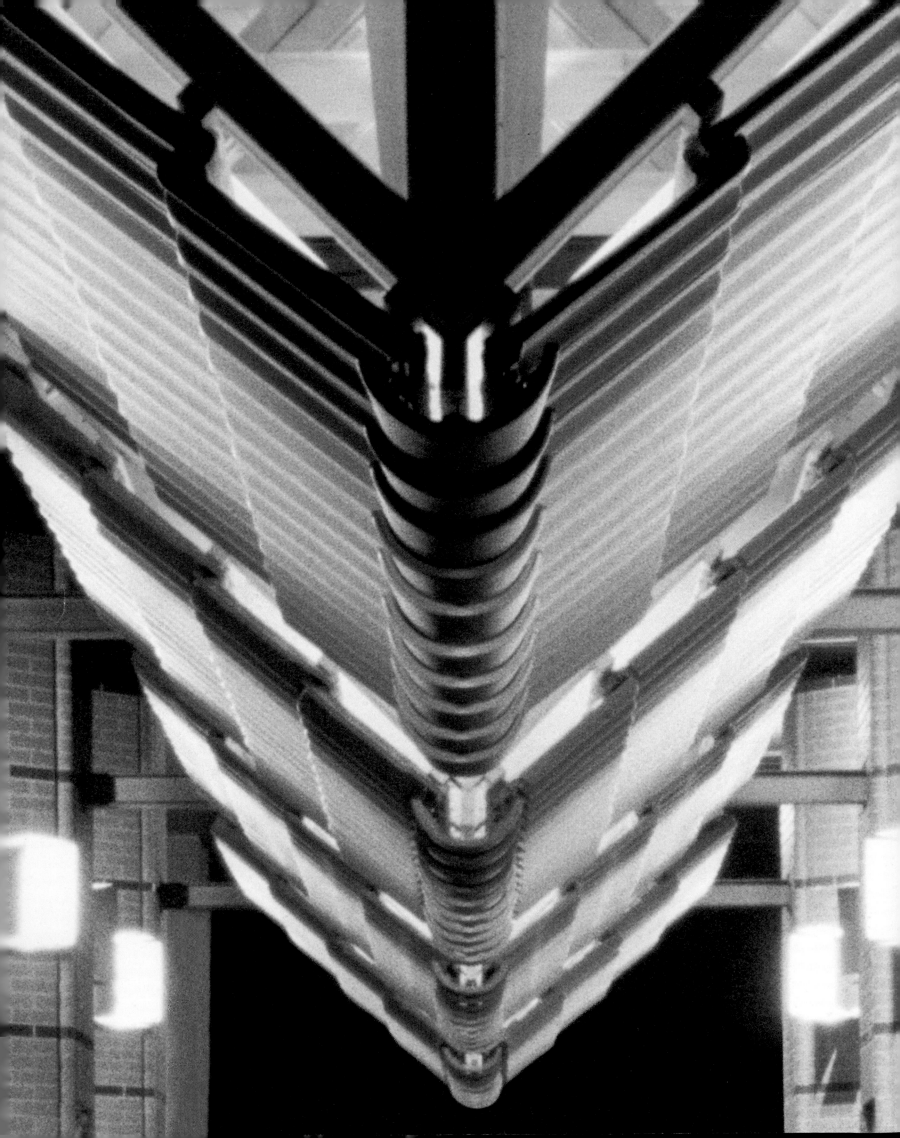

How does a building materials company get across the diverse uses of its products?

ZZ, Zürcher Ziegeleien
Swissbau, Basel 1987

Reinhard designed the stand for Zürcher Ziegeleien for the Swissbau show in Basel for the first time in 1987. The 150 square metre stand is framed by six brick columns containing showcases with the company's decorative products. A roof gable mounted upside-down floats above the central aisle – trade information and eye-catcher in one. The beam structure is reflected kaleidoscopically. Prefabricated elements permit rapid assembly and mean that the stand can be reused. Zürcher Ziegeleien always likes to spring a surprise with a new stand design at the biennial building show, as a means of demonstrating the firm's highly creative approach.

front view

section

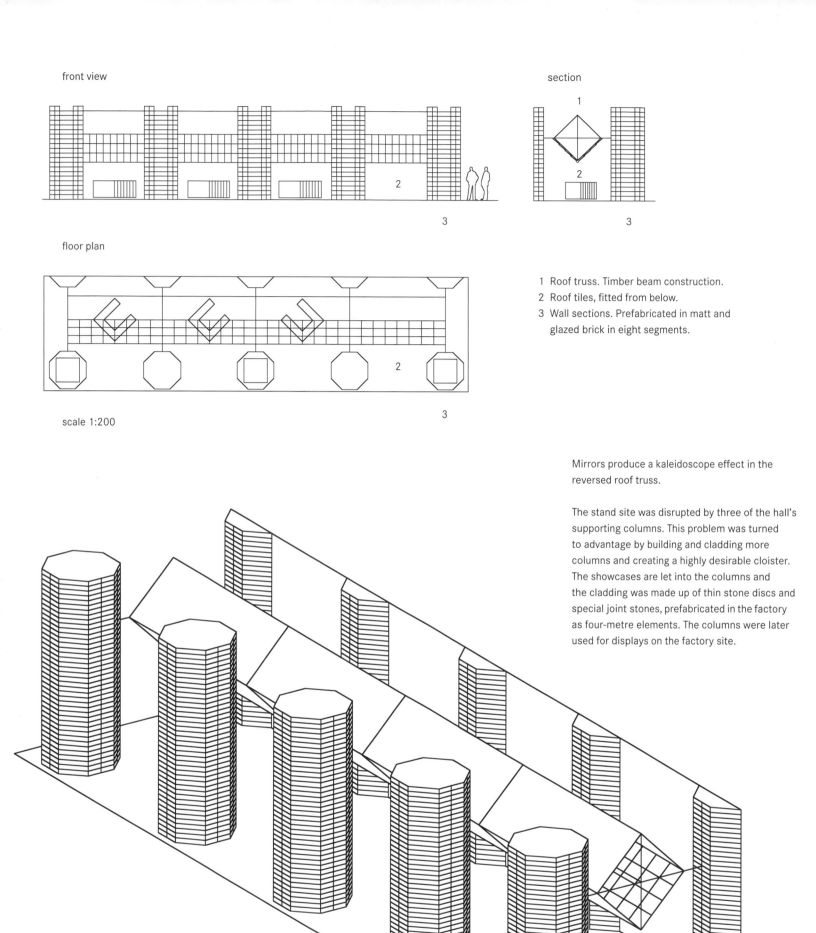

floor plan

1 Roof truss. Timber beam construction.
2 Roof tiles, fitted from below.
3 Wall sections. Prefabricated in matt and
  glazed brick in eight segments.

scale 1:200

Mirrors produce a kaleidoscope effect in the
reversed roof truss.

The stand site was disrupted by three of the hall's
supporting columns. This problem was turned
to advantage by building and cladding more
columns and creating a highly desirable cloister.
The showcases are let into the columns and
the cladding was made up of thin stone discs and
special joint stones, prefabricated in the factory
as four-metre elements. The columns were later
used for displays on the factory site.

Transfor

mations

Fundamentally there are two kinds of exhibition stand: disposable stands and reusable stands. Disposable stands look old after they have been used once and are then dismantled and 'disposed of', which is one problem less for the person who built it, but one problem more for the host city or state which has to get rid of the rubbish. Reusable stands are good enough to survive a number of appearances. They are often conceived in such a way that they can be adapted to new circumstances. They do not produce huge quantities of special rubbish, and are a long-term investment.

Flexibility in a stand means long life, and in turn this is good for costs and ecology. A system using standard parts means that every stand can be changed into another one, or so the current view would have it. But appearances are deceptive. System construction alone does not produce flexibility, as construction alone does not make a stand. Only a very few stand systems, developed in a very sophisticated way, with variable elements for primary construction and diverse secondary elements – displays, lighting, furnishing – fulfil the requirement of variability at a high level of design. But they always have the disadvantage that ultimately they do not fulfil individual needs. They also need a great deal of storage space and demand more components than are ever used in the end. And something they can do only with great difficulty is to make an unmistakable contribution to the exhibitor's company identity. To an extent the standardized system thrusts itself in front of the image that the company intends to create. Thus standardized systems have their limitations. They are best suited for exhibition construction firms who have to do large numbers of jobs that do not make great demands in terms of design. If corporate design is an important factor then the standard system will very rarely be adequate.

Tailor-made systems

Anyone trying to solve this problem will have to develop an individual system. This offers the advantage that the specific requirements of a presentation can be included from the outset. As a rule this produces solutions that help to shape the firm's identity. Here neither the size of the company nor the size of the stand is crucial. In fact tailor-made systems can be particularly useful for small-scale appearances. Edgar Reinhard has produced large-scale systems for IBM and Toyota as well as various smaller schemes. One example of this is the stand for Silent Gliss, 1994 (see illustration in Chapter one). On the Silent Gliss stand show containers for textiles and slide rails form system units. One or more units can be set up according to the size of the presentation. This can be done very quickly by the use of simply fitted supports. The containers are also transport units, which can be stocked up before the show. Cabling is also prefabricated and integrated. The iron and steel used for the primary structure are so durable that the stand can be used several times a year over a long period without any difficulty. Flexibility can also mean that only the exterior is changed for a new show. Thus the stand for the Neue Zürcher Zeitung was used at the same trade fair for several years, but with a different basic colour for the structure each year. Additional slight modifications made the stand seem new each time. The long half-life offered by a 'reticent' design was appropriate to the image of this conservative paper.

Spaceship three times different

Reinhard transformed the stand for IBM for Telecom 1987, 1991 and 1995 in quite different dimensions, in terms of both space and content. The floating body, reminiscent of a spaceship, had a sensational effect over eight years because the concept was so simple and manageable: a floating box that could be filled and decorated in different ways. Of course the box looked special, it was like a modern magic chest, a mysterious shrine, inside which inconceivable things must be taking place.

Technically IBM's range changed so much in this period that the interior design was almost completely different from show to show. The system concept allowed these adaptations without difficulty, not least thanks to anticipatory planning, for example in terms of fitting thousands of kilometres of cable. On its third appearance the planks of the floating container glittered with thousands of points of light: the stars of the Milky Way. This decorative trick had the right effect – the enormous investment paid its way for a third time. If one calculates the multiple-use over many years of a stand owned by the firm itself, it is ultimately no more expensive or even cheaper than a bought or rented standard solution.

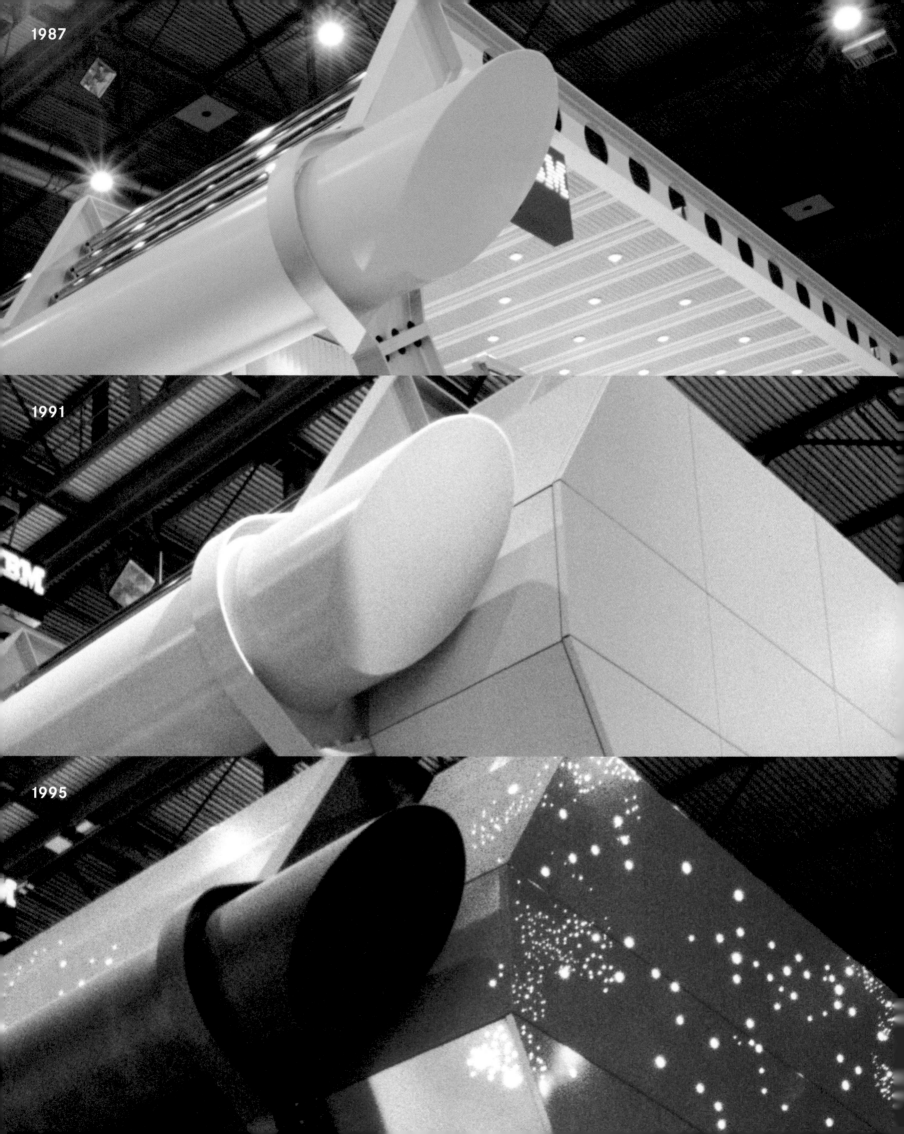

1987

1991

1995

How does the exhibitor account for the rapid change of the telecoms market?

IBM
World Exhibition of Telecommunications
Geneva 1987, 1991, 1995

The 1987 IBM stand was varied in different ways, technically, visually and in terms of use for 1991 and 1995. The basic concept proved excellently suited to this approach. The most striking external variation was a new anchoring system. In 1987 the stand was supported by four corner piers. From 1991 it was suspended on four centrally positioned diagonal piers, which considerably enhanced the impression of floating and made for more flexible use of the ground floor. The major structural investment in the foundations meant that IBM was also able to secure its very good position in the hall for 1995.

The second striking change was an additional floor for offices. Exhibition areas on four levels were reached by lift and generous staircases. The third floor was reserved for VIP receptions and the press. A 100-seat theatre was provided, and visitors could choose between six languages with an infra-red device. On the threshold of the 1990s, the telecommunications market was developing explosively. This was reflected by trade fair stands that progressively competed with each other in size. In 1987, the IBM stand was the sensation of the show in terms of size, but by its third appearance it looked positively modest alongside the now multi-storey stands of other global companies. But in terms of design the IBM stand turned out to be a jewel when compared with competing 'excrescences' which had no underlying concept. The shell's planking was now strewn with the stars of the Milky Way from the northern evening sky. Each star glowed as a fibre-optically controlled point of light – 370 transformers were used, each feeding 100 glass fibres.

At the stand's appearances from 1987, there were no product presentations at all. IBM's competence in this field was taken for granted. So IBM machines were present simply as functional terminals. The actual 'product' being advertised was IBM's competence in system solutions.

'Data Highway', 'World Wide Web', 'Internet' – these are the technology bywords of the 1990s. IBM was ready for this, with their sales maxim 'Solutions rather than products'. Appropriately there were no experts on the stand in 1995 – the job was taken over by professional actors who were specially trained and flown in from the USA. There were, however, 200 IBM experts needed for the preparations, to set up the necessary technical centre in a nearby underground car-park and cable it to the stand.

According to a survey of the public by an independent institution, the stand was very highly rated. Yet the average cost per visitor was no higher than for other stands in the same sector.

1987

1995

Stage 2

Networking
Solutions
for Network
Operators

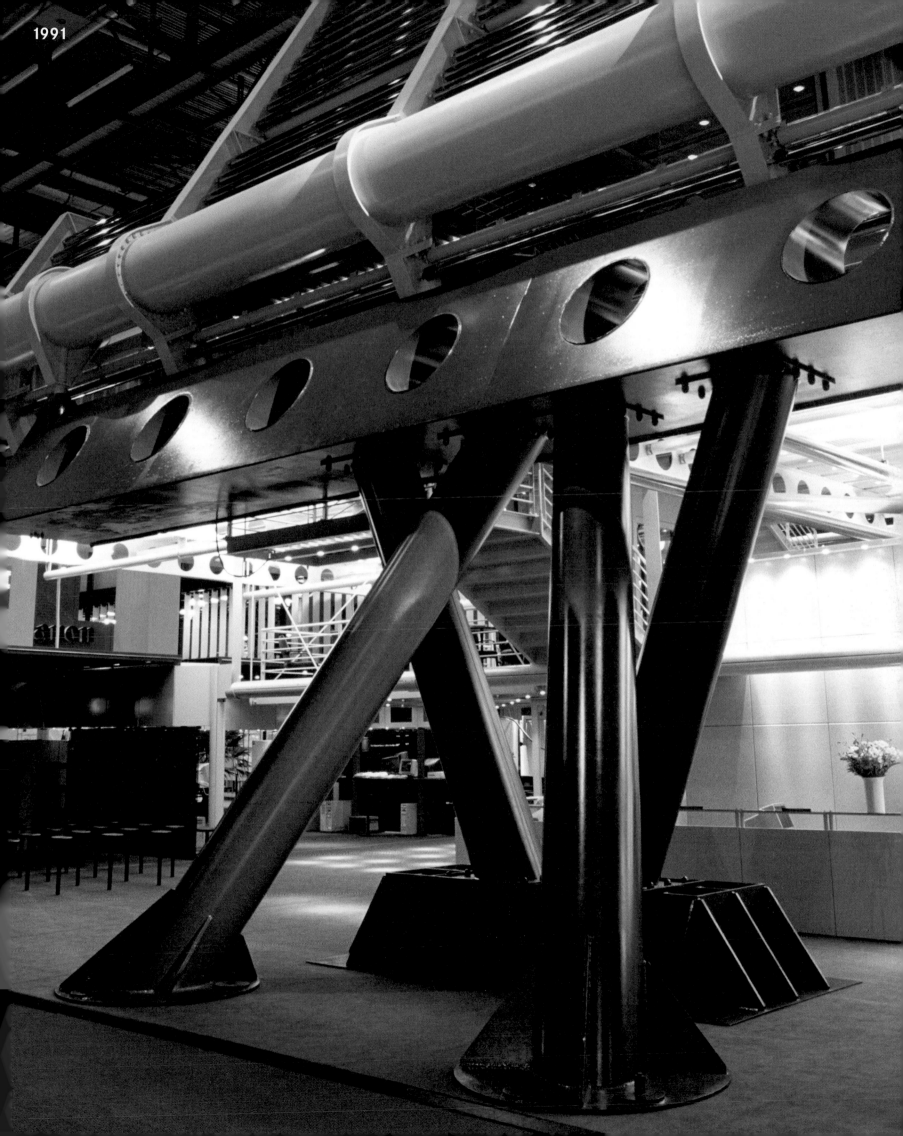

side view

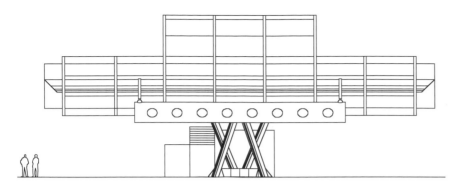

front view

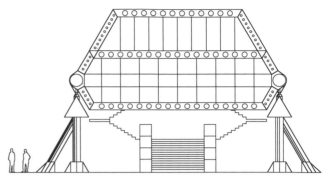

floor plan

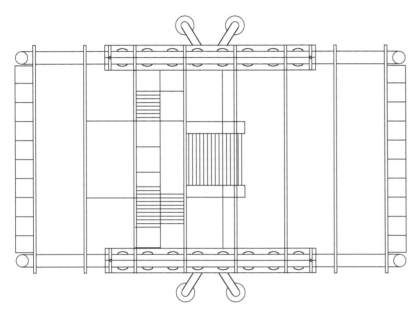

scale 1:300

In 1987 the pavilion was supported by four corner piers; from 1991 by the two central column groups. This not only reinforced the effect of floating, but also meant that the floor area could be used more flexibly. And because of the floor anchorages, the stand was also able to secure a prominent place in the hall.

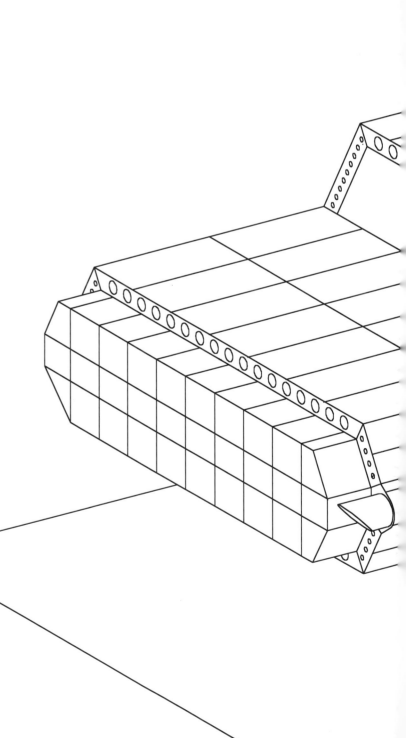

Telecom 1987

1 Four concrete stays.
2 Replaced and raised by two steel stays
  mounted on a ground tie 17 metres deep.
3 Central steps, leading to the two upper
  floors via an intermediate platform.
4 Second floor built on top.
5 Intermediate platform at 2.6 metres.

front view   side view

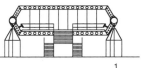
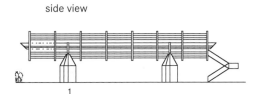

1   1

Telecom 1991, 1995

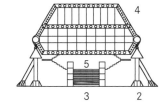
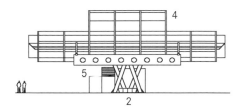

4   4

5   5

3   2   2

scale 1:600

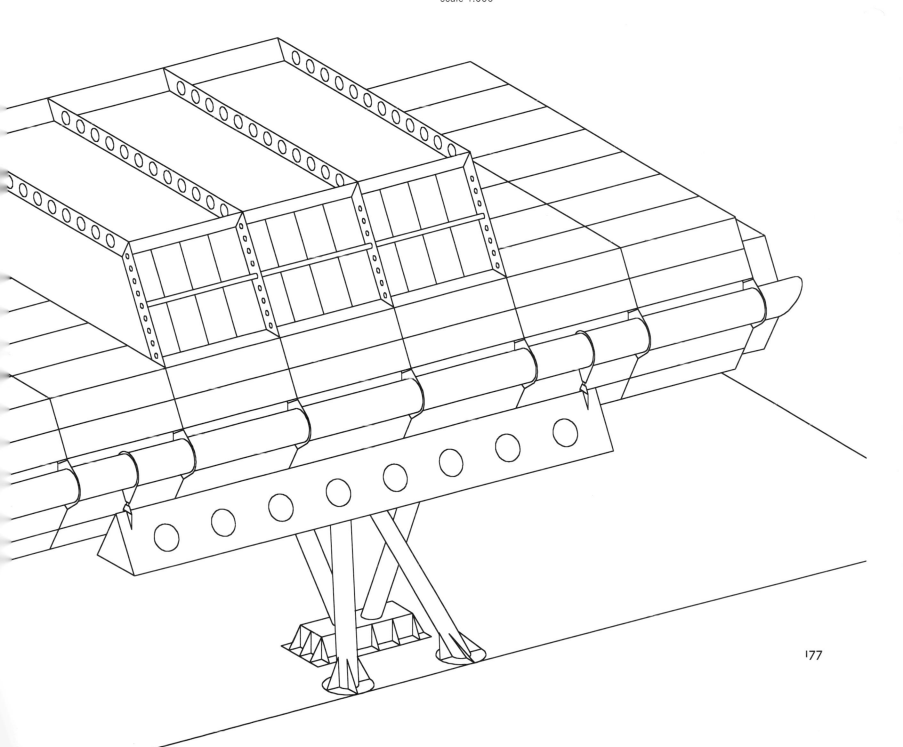

The 'Milky Way' motif can be experienced outside as well as in the interior.

The more emotional 1995 lighting concept corresponds with the constellations on the outer shell. In l991 the lighting was arranged in a direct and linear fashion.

Even the meeting rooms on the executive level were furnished more emotionally in 1995.

A generous reception area and a 100-seat projection room met the prime communication requirement from 1991 (1995 version shown).

How does a world-class newspaper show itself to potential readers?

NZZ, Neue Zürcher Zeitung
Basel 1984 – 1991

This stand was used at the Muba public trade fair in different variants, with the colouring most notably changed annually. Skeleton-like stands, or 'robots', serve as newspaper-holders and eye-catchers. The artificial newspaper readers hold questionnaires, which visitors can use to test their knowledge in the fields of culture, politics and economics. This interaction has parallels with an advertising campaign.

The stand was set up by two men in two days. The newspaper-stand figures were used again at the Frankfurt Book Fair in 1995 and 1996.

School classes went through the course as part of their media training. The intention was to bring young people closer to the medium of print in the television age.

Visitors evaluated their own questionnaires and took part in a raffle.

section   front view

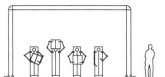

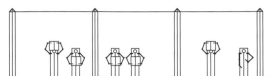

floor plan

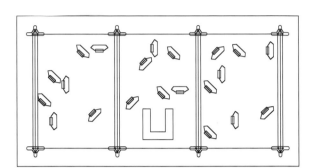

The structural part of the stand was   1 Loudspeakers, which started to operate
coloured differently and the display,   in random sequence.
a set of questions, was changed.   2 Spine feeding the sound signals.

scale 1:200

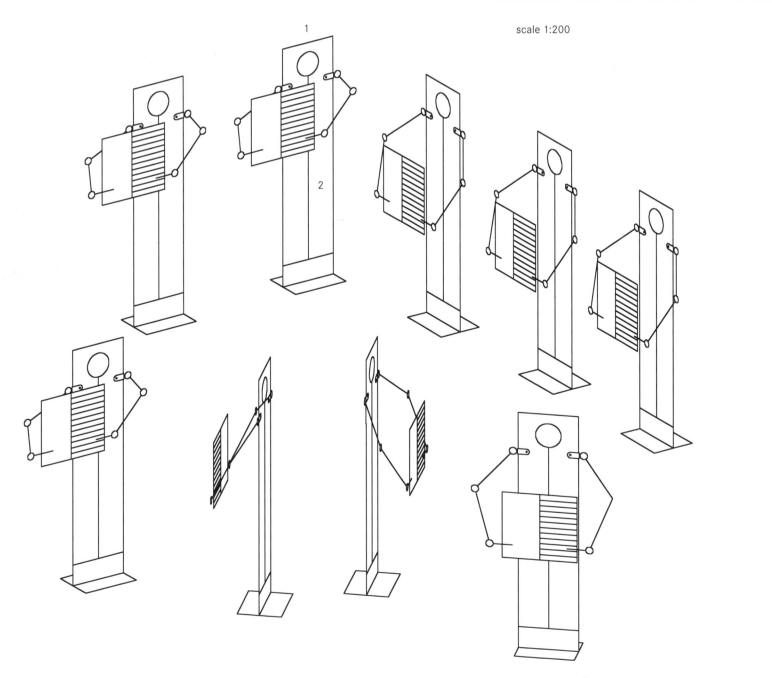

Material &

Construction

In the last 40 years the material world of trade fairs has changed considerably. In the 1960s there were only a few standard systems, whereas today there is a large competing range from the simplest scaffolding construction kits to highly sophisticated modular systems for variable interiors. But individual stands and systems have also adapted to new conditions. First high-tech is all the rage, then it's back to lively little parties and then the new cosiness of the 1990s.

System building for trade fairs was generally discovered in the 1960s, with sheet-iron profiles setting the tone. In the 1970s aluminium profiles appeared, in fact aluminium was the quintessential high-tech material. The 1980s design boom did not stop at trade fairs. 'Experience' stands were all the rage, but things could just not be sufficiently solidly made: chromium steel, glass, granite and marble conjured a world of glitter and distinction into the halls. In the 1990s it has been clear that there is a move away from expensive materials – concept and processing have become the key factors. People are not afraid of using timber and cardboard even when promoting high-tech products. Paper, fabrics, wood – these preferred materials of the 1990s avant-garde stands are warm and soft, pleasant to the touch. Cosiness is the new trend. Of course these materials, particularly wood, are expensive to process and give only limited wear. And although they seem ecologically sound at first glance, research should be done into whether this really is the case.

Eco-balance required

Without drawing up an eco-balance for the whole life of a stand it is scarcely possible to make viable statements about actual environmental friendliness. For example, an aluminium stand swallows huge quantities of electricity when the metal is manufactured, so-called grey energy. The balance, however, swings in its favour the more the stand is used, although transport appears on the negative side. Materials like wood or semi-finished products like fibre-board, or the most typical materials that wear out such as carpets and other floor coverings are scarcely ever used more than once for trade fairs. They tend to be burned after their first appearance. An ecologically impeccable natural fibre carpet in coconut or sisal can be burned with fewer side effects once it is on the rubbish dump than can a carpet made of artificial fibre. Whether it is more environmentally friendly overall would have to be worked out later – it probably is, if both kinds are used only once.

Considerations of this kind are rare in the trade fair business. In this respect the trade fair stand has something of a carnival quality about it: colourful fireworks along with the high-life, quickly burnt out, consumed and off to the dump with it. But as the piles of rubbish grow, trade fair organizers have gone over to a stricter regime of rubbish handling, with more or less keen checks on material flow and disposal. Under this pressure ecology is now included in the concept of the stand here and there. Although one just as frequently sees impressive stands being chopped into little pieces or dismantled with welding torches, no matter what they are made of.

Exhibition design: reflecting a lifestyle
Mere technology can increasingly manage without symbols of this kind. Arnold Schwarzenegger and his 'technoid' phantasms are bound to be less fascinating in future, and thus less appealing from day to day. Technology is no longer appealing as such, but we are fascinated by the fact that it can make life so pleasant and give us so many tantalising glimpses of the farthest corners of the world. At the same time, as work is in increasingly short supply, the leisure industry is growing apace. Sex and fun are permanent ingredients of urban life, even if they are only appearances. And this affects the construction of trade fairs as well. Things are not up to much without atmospheric appurtenances, whether they be real or fake. But the quality of eventfulness that we have already discussed has become more sophisticated. Signals are sent to potential clients by balanced interior design, ingenious installations, subtle lighting, etc. And so more and more experts trained in design have to be involved. Old trade fair hands engage young, freelance professionals for a particular project: they have their ears to the ground and are not bogged down in the customary practices of the trade fair industry. Or trade fair firms, if they are big enough, engage 'art directors', who are able to co-ordinate various design experts – graphics, product, stand architecture – with those responsible for marketing.

Materials, construction and design in the work of Edgar Reinhard

Seen this way, Edgar Reinhard's working style has been overtaken by the times. As a freelance designer he never had to submit to the dictates of concepts, material or construction, but always fixed them himself and convinced his clients about them. Here he played the role of the general contractor from time to time, holding all the threads in his hand, from engineer to graphic designer.

In terms of material technology, Reinhard's stands show an intelligent frugality. He takes semi-finished products from the building industry and uses them to design high-calibre elements (IBM Telecom 1979), or has a pavilion made in steel in the conventional manner (IBM Telecom 1983), although designed in such a futuristic way that it was used as a pavilion outside trade fairs for many years afterwards. For an aluminium firm he built aluminium into a stand so convincingly that the advantages of the material can be seen from some distance away (Alusuisse, Belgrade 1972). I could give more examples. After economy, the lucidity of the construction is the major feature. Reinhard does not offer us any decorative, non-functional baubles. One glance is enough, and we know what we have before us. This utterly honest and completely self-confident approach lends the exhibits something that was the Swiss hallmark for years: solidity and quality. But this solidity never seems stolid or dull. On the contrary, there is always a dash of elegance or sophistication involved, for example the constructive care behind the TV stage set for the Karussell programme seems solid and of high quality. But the construction does not force itself into the foreground or even put the product in the shade – the stand architecture retains its service character; it is present and trenchant, but not dominant.

In particularly successful cases the material quality becomes part of the product message – for example in the plastic cathedral for Dow Chemicals in 1971 where the vulnerable cover indicates the danger presented by the water, in the stands for Zürcher Ziegeleien, in the fibre-optic cable logo for the Rieter spinning machine company, in the above-mentioned stand for the aluminium industry and others.

Reusability

A central and recurrent theme is reusability and structural systematics (see also previous chapter). Reinhard's work is consistently designed for reuse and ease of transformation. He does not design trade fair stands, but stand systems, tailored to the client's product and company language. Metal is his preferred material because it is simple to use and to adapt, and because it is durable and stable. The metal box form comes up for pavilions and furniture, and also for skeleton construction (the tent again!).

Installations

There is another group of works with installation as a common feature (Dow Chemical 1970/1971/1973/1979; Zürcher Ziegeleien, Swissbau 1987/1993/1995; ADC 1982; Roche Duftkarussell 1996). Like the system structures, they rely a great deal on analogy. The need to illustrate invisible chemical processes and reagents or even sets of facts in their context led to a series of symbolic solutions with strong visual signs. Plastic granules welded into suspended strips of transparent cloth, a labyrinth of piled up barrels, an inflated cathedral with water-cushions on the floor, light playing on shop-window dummies, etc. – realizations like this are as entertaining as an artistic installation, but also convey information and evoke memories. Edgar Reinhard does not like his trade fair installations to be discussed as if they were art. They are scarcely inferior to artistic installations in the way they accurately express an aspect of the times. The principal distinction lies in their affirmative character. Reinhard puts himself entirely at the service of the client. An artist would not have been able to allow himself to represent Dow Chemical, a producer of chemical warfare agents, in a highly aesthetic way so shortly after the Vietnam trauma.

An aluminium company looks best in aluminium.

**Alusuisse
Belgrade 1972**

This aluminium structure was designed specially for the exhibition in Belgrade. In this way the aesthetics and functional qualities of the material could best be tuned to the aluminium producer's self-representation. The closed-looking, lavishly proportioned exterior lures visitors inside, where an abundance of products, textual information and video films await them.

Only semi-finished products were used – and simple processes like chamfering and screwing together. The display was subsequently taken to Yugoslavia, where Alusuisse organized exhibitions as a device for transferring technology to the third world.

front view

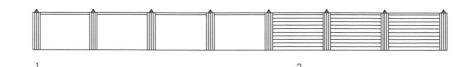

1   2

1

floor plan

2

1 Support structure. Naturally anodized   scale 1:300
   aluminium, screwed.
2 Wall, ceiling cladding. Aluminium
   trapezium profile.

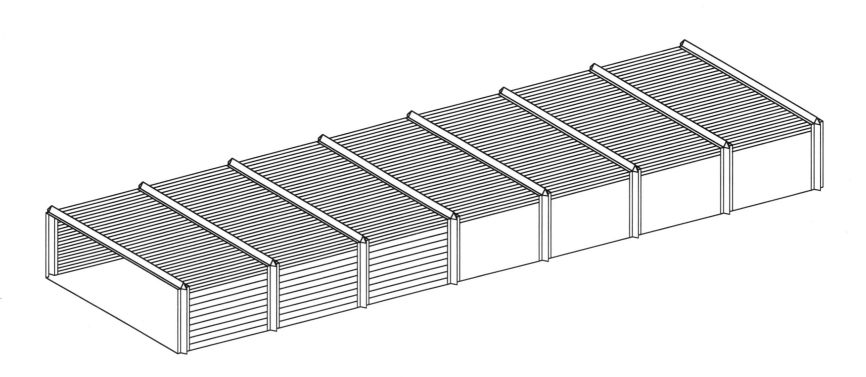

ALUSUISSE

THIS EXHIBITION STAND COVERS
400 SQUARE METERS. IT WAS
DESIGNED, DELIVERED AND
ERECTED IN BELGRADE AS A
TURNKEY JOB BY EDGAR REINHARD.

Décor is not always decoration.

Swiss Television
'Karussell' stage set 1983

The décor for Swiss Television's 'Karussell' programme consisted essentially of system stands and perforated aluminium panels. The intelligible structure and ability to change rapidly established the quality of this system.
'Karussel' was a magazine programme that was broadcast daily for many years. Ease of conversion was intended to encourage the directors to adapt the décor to the programme. Light projections through the shadow masks in the panels made a wide range of textures and colour combinations possible. The principle was used by Constructivists in the 1920s for stage sets – a late homage from a different medium.

front, rectangular setup

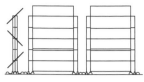

front, diagonal setup

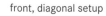

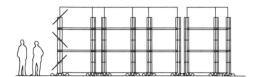

floor plan

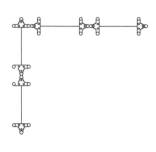

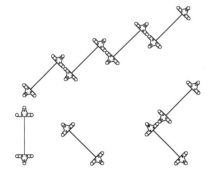

Various ways of piercing the sheets, different lighting and arrangements made it possible to achieve a range of effects in the shortest possible time. Thus the management could adapt the décor to the most up-to-date requirements within hours. The pierced holes worked as masking for the coloured spotlights.
The projected dots and stripes produced moiré effects and overlapping colours.

scale 1 : 200

1 Mobile casting feet.
2 Stays. Aluminium tubes with extruded aluminium connecting elements.
3 Swivelling perforated plates in various sizes and arrangements.

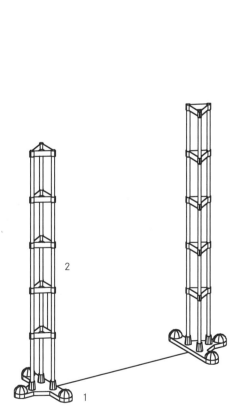

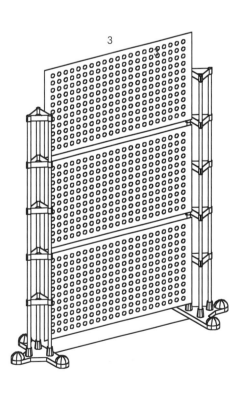

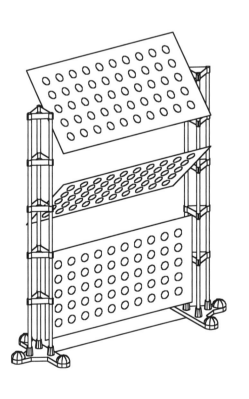

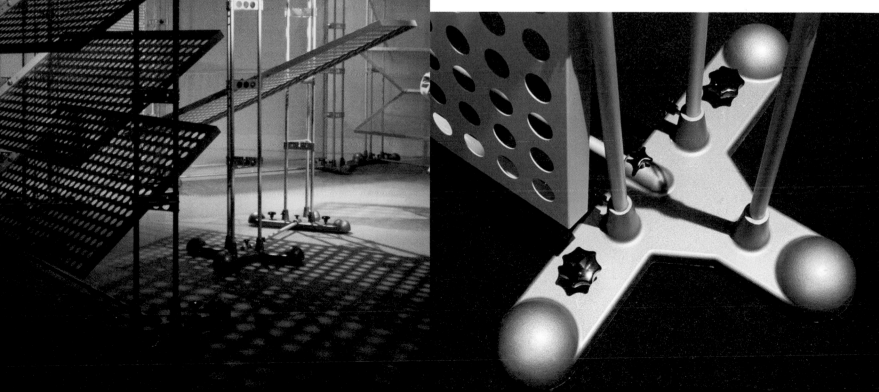

You can show more of yourself with a stand of your own.

IBM

**Stand system for Swiss trade fairs,
1984–1991**

IBM Switzerland used its own stand system from 1984–
91. Unlike Telecom Geneva, which was an image and strategy show, this stand was used at sales shows. The protruding horizontal-vertical elements and the coloured emphasis of the junctions were the particular characteristics.
The stand infrastructure has to allow equipment to be connected up at the last minute. The skirting board of the partition walls was used as a cabling channel. Pre-cabling and perforation were geared to Local Area Network plugs, and meant that 220 volt electrical connections were available wherever needed. The cables ran along the covered main girders.

The stay pipes (top and left) have shells to take the cabling. The walls can be turned and adjusted as required. The ceiling elements can be fitted with various lamps, such as spots and floods, and also allow stale air to escape.

front view

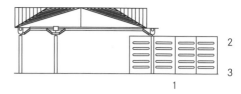

side view

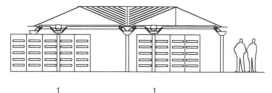

layout variations

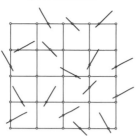

floor plan

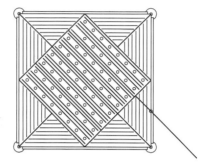

scale 1:200

floor plan

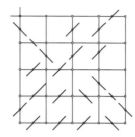

scale 1 : 1000

1 Stay with adapter for attachment to supply channels as required.
2 Polyester wall elements. Hollow for running cables.
3 Floor tracks with power sockets for all requirements.

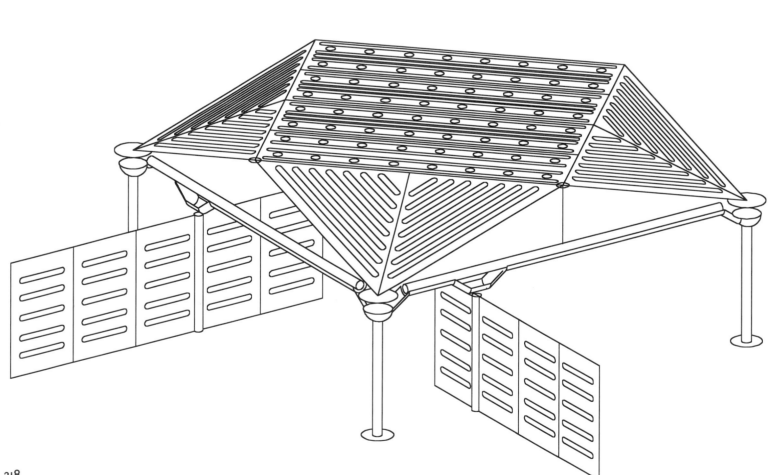

It doesn't always have to be marble, stone and stainless steel.

IBM
World Exhibition of Telecommunications
Geneva 1979

IBM registered late for this first communications world fair in Geneva and was thus allotted five small stand areas. Reinhard made them into a unit by roofing them with a grid-like channel system.

The reflectors mounted on this are reminiscent of solar panels, and the grid construction of satellites. At the time IBM's main concern was to sell terminals, so the futuristic, emphatically technological appearance stressed the company's technical competence. In later stand concepts for IBM (1983-95) the technological aspect of the terminals shifted further into the background.

As only three months were available for planning, readily available semi-finished products had to be used for the construction. Iron grids were employed for the main section and galvanized sheets for the consoles that are almost sculptural in character. Live birch hedges were used as a contrast to the cool structure; their leaves changed to autumn colours in the course of the ten-day exhibition.

The example shows how the construction method itself can achieve a powerful effect using rudimentary materials.

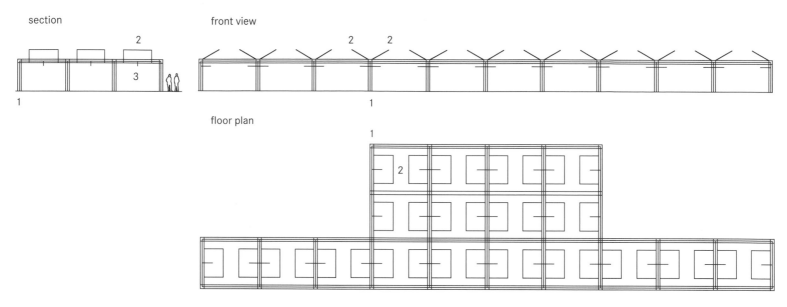

section

front view

2   2

floor plan

1

2

scale 1:400

1 Grid structure with internal cable
   channels.
2 Reflector for indirect lighting of the
   work-stations with monitors.
3 Light with connection to the cable
   channel.

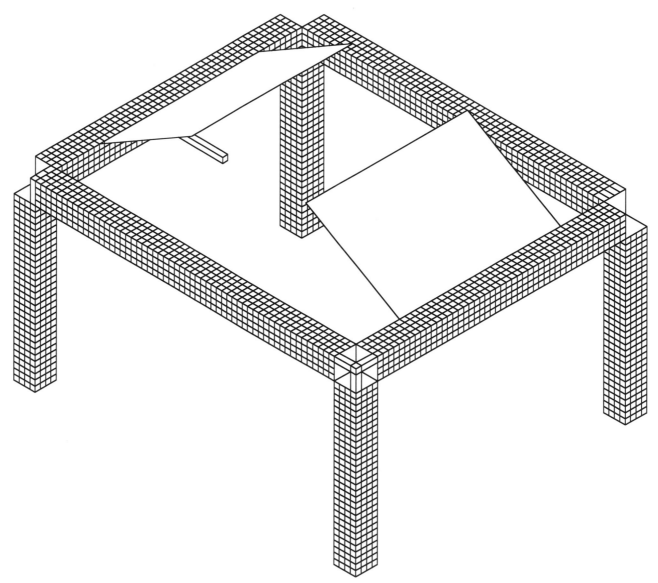

Computers still had very little significance at this 1979 exhibition. The diagonally placed aluminium reflectors evoked images of space probes equipped with solar cells – representative of technical progress at the time. The support structure needs only a few simple elements. The junctions are welded together from three steel angles. The cables run through the grid channels.

How does a market leader position itself in a new market?

IBM
World Exhibition of Telecommunications
Geneva 1983

This pavilion, apparently floating in the open air like a 'landing module', stands on impressive corner columns, which are emphasized both structurally and in terms of colour. The artificial landscape is a mound of pebbles – the earth is opening up, something new is coming out of the ground.

The small, open modules for the individual divisions of the company are grouped around the second pavilion inside the hall. The diagonally placed wooden panels are covered with quartz sand and contain the infrastructure for lighting, sound and electricity. Customer information is provided at these modules, and the pavilion is used for film performances and as an exhibition area.

The pavilions were produced by a steel and façade construction company employing conventional steel erection techniques, mainly using industry-standard, semi-finished products. The detailed design, for instance the column connections and roof drainage, presented the engineers with problems that a normal exhibition stand company would not be expected to solve.

The stand caused a considerable stir among the public and in the trade, and kept Reinhard one jump ahead of his fellow competitors for further IBM shows (1987/91/95) at Telecom Geneva.

The pavilions were handed over to a transportation systems company after the fair, who dismantled them free of charge and has since used them as showrooms.

The module in the open air seems to be rising up over the broken earth – the birth of a new generation of products.

The module in the hall contains a projection room, with an exhibition about the manufacture of computer chips behind it. Ceiling-high columns carry staggered displays of the original miniature parts.

Every IBM division has a sound-proof outside element at its disposal. The floor and the V-elements are coated with quartz sand, continuing the stone/earth theme of the open-air presentation.

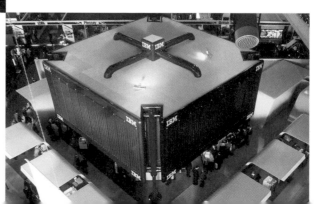

231

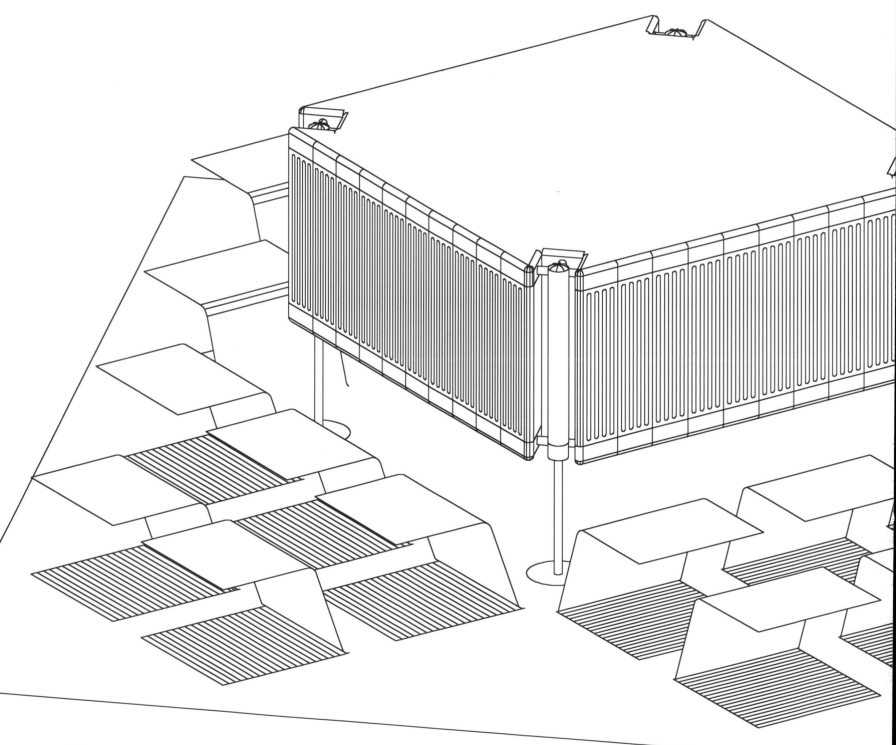

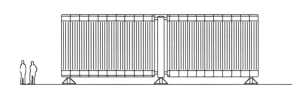
pavilion outside

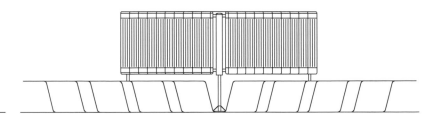
stand inside exhibition hall

floor plan

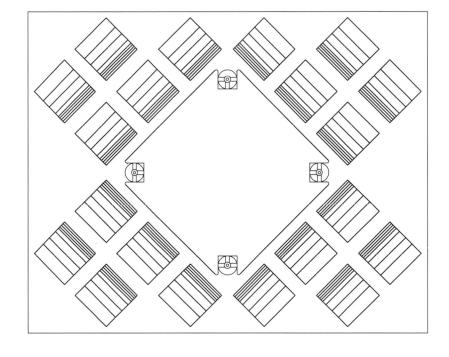

scale 1:300

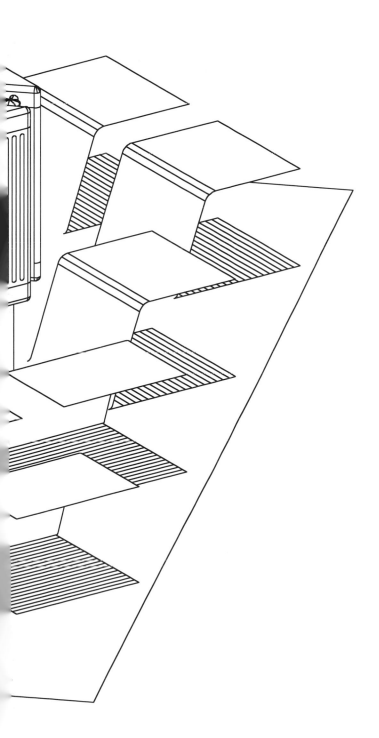

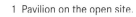

1 Pavilion on the open site.
2 Pavilion with theatre and exhibition area
  in the hall.
3 Demonstration modules. Exterior quartz
  sand, interior sound-absorbent material.
  In the cavity – light, sound, technical
  installations.

How to prevent the stand from stealing the show from the exhibits?

Planmöbel
Orgatec, Cologne 1992, 1994, 1996

The modular structure is in untreated, uncoated steel profiles and galvanized, punched sheets which provide a contrast to the high-tech furniture presented. The openly fitted perforated sheets allow optimum lighting design with low-voltage downlighters.

The system aims at the best possible lighting for the furniture that is being displayed, and is not intended to compete with it visually. The same elements are used for the ceiling and dividing walls. The three round units contain a prototype show for a selected audience, a meeting room, a kitchen and storage facilities.

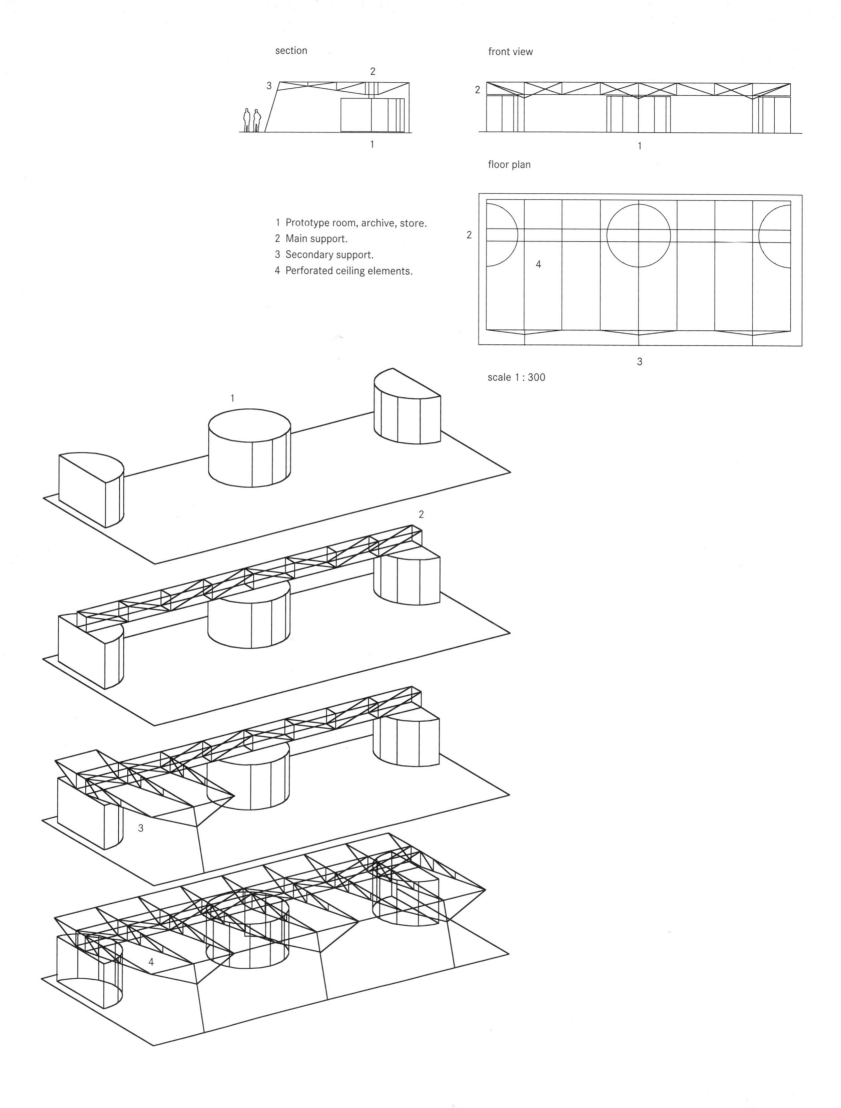

section

front view

3   2

2

1

2

1

floor plan

4

3

1 Prototype room, archive, store.
2 Main support.
3 Secondary support.
4 Perforated ceiling elements.

scale 1 : 300

1

2

3

4

How art directors allow themselves to be seen.

**Art Directors Club of Switzerland
City Hall, Zurich 1982**

For a self-presentation by the Art Directors Club at the Stadthaus in Zurich, Reinhard, who is a member of the board, fitted out the internal arcades on the light-well side with a display system. In this way, as soon as visitors came through the main door on the ground floor, their attention was drawn to the exhibition in the upper storeys. The ADC wanted to use this exhibition to enhance the organization's public profile. Interest was aroused by the large colour panels on entering the hall – a striking contrast with the architecture of the building. Visitors could turn their attention to the material without interruption in the lobbies.

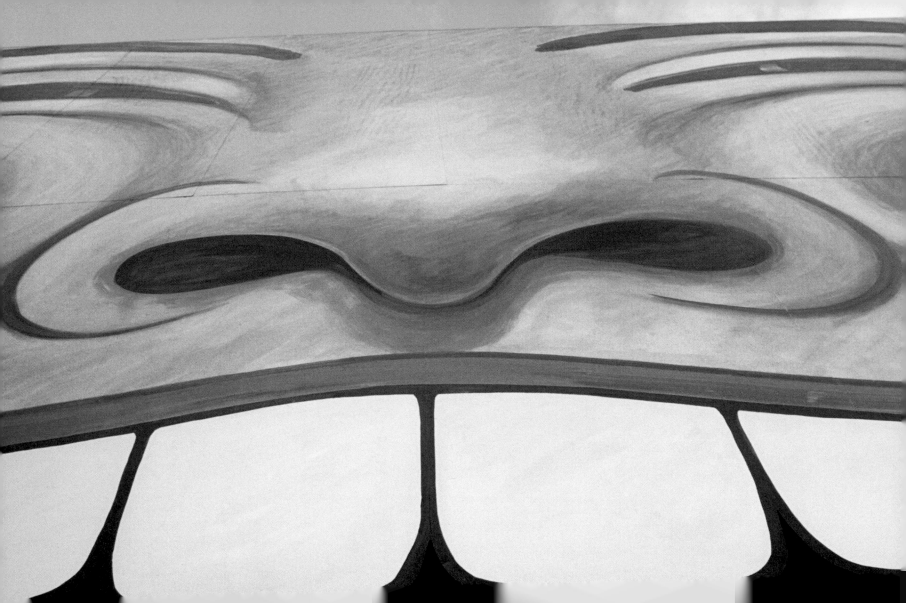

Sometimes you can even smell competence...

**Hoffmann La Roche
Basel 1996**

The Basel-based chemical company Roche organized a public exhibition including various spectacles for its 100th anniversary. In Reinhard's Duftkarussell, or Fragrance Roundabout, the visitors drove through a black tunnel with several different fragrance zones to an acoustic accompaniment on headphones. There was a sequence of aromas of coffee, perfume, soap, sports cream, etc, staggered like the events of a day.

The individual fragrance zones were separated only by air curtains, which required some finesse from the air conditioning engineers. An elaborate ventilation plant took the perfumed air to and from the individual fragrance zones, which were divided from each other by air curtains. Compensation was also needed for the air circulation caused by the carousel.

The sound accompaniment had to be precisely synchronised. Battery-powered CD players provided sound for two seats each and a load-controlled hydraulic motor kept the speed constant. Reinhard took this presentation to the limits of technical feasibility.

side view

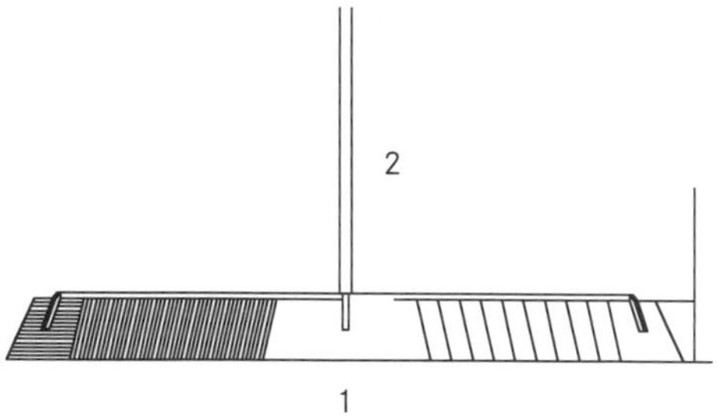

front view

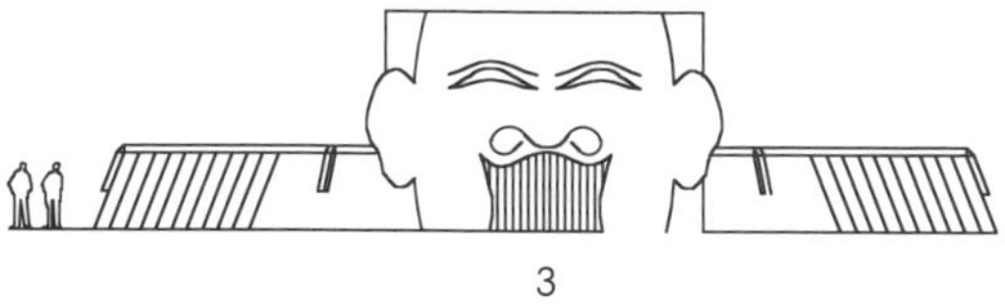

floor plan

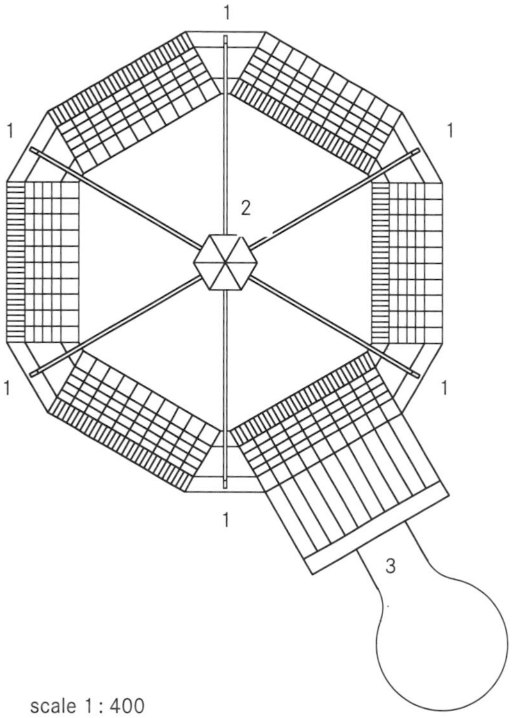

1 Round course with supply for fragrance zones.
2 Central ventilation or aromatization plant.
3 Visitors go through the entrance air-lock into
  an almost completely blacked-out access area.
  Separate entrance and exit.

The ducts for incoming and outgoing air are
controlled from the centre of the circuit.
Once visitors have entered the fairground-like
tunnel they are in a closed system.

scale 1 : 400

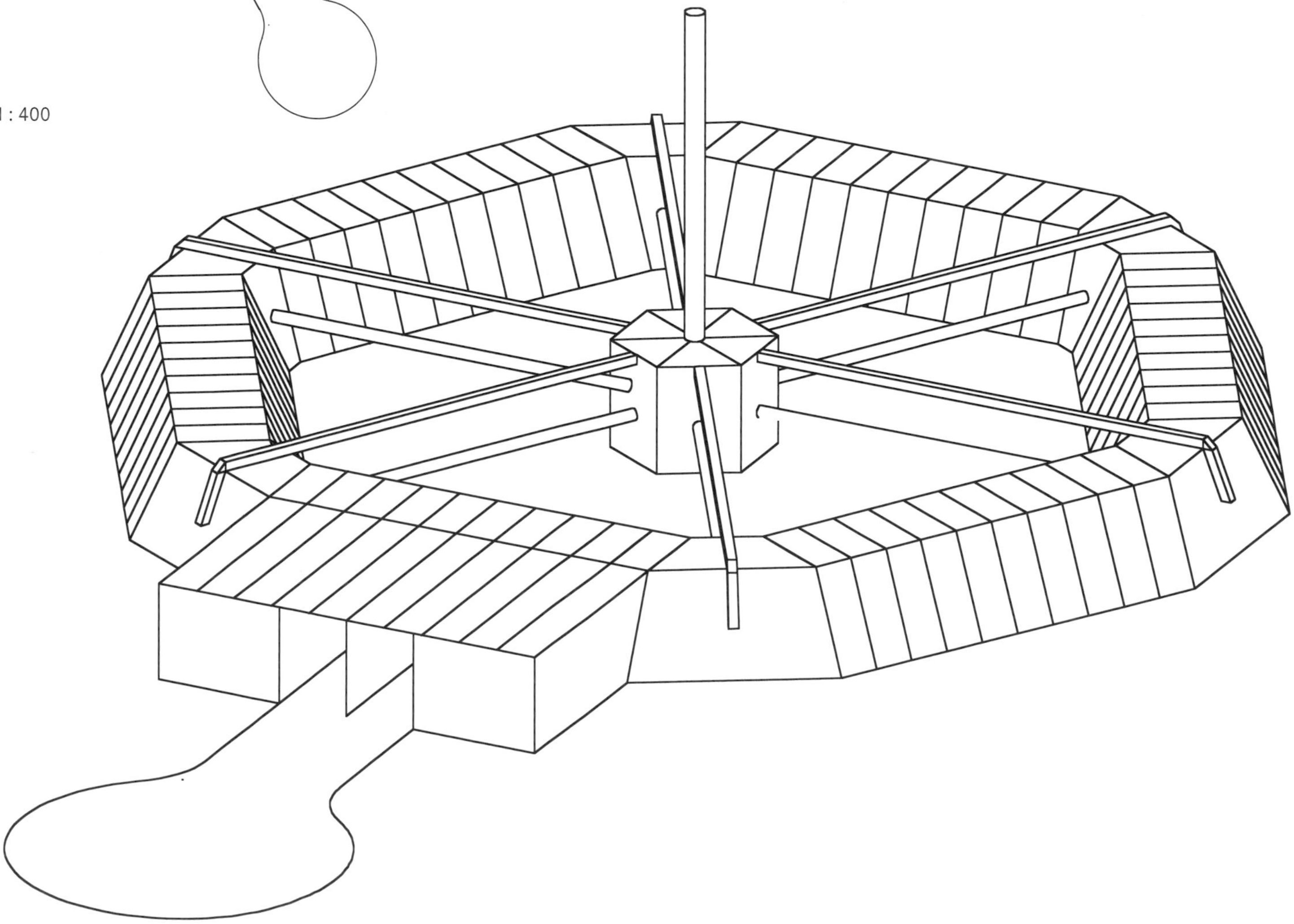

Battery-powered CD players provide sound for each pair of visitors' seats.

An important part of the game: trade fair furniture.

A meeting room does not need new furniture invented for it. But where the furniture becomes an important part of the presentation then its function, and thus its form, can be tailor-made. That form follows function, the dictum of Classical Modernism, has lost none of its meaning in the world of trade fairs. Reinhard's furniture addresses its purpose, which does not prevent it from being beautiful. It is a beauty arising from rational construction, sometimes with a sculptural character.

Round counter for Silent Gliss.

Round counter for IBM Telecom 1995.

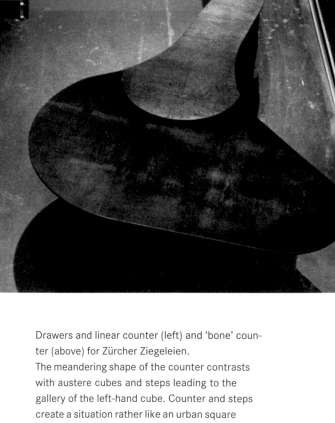

Drawers and linear counter (left) and 'bone' counter (above) for Zürcher Ziegeleien.
The meandering shape of the counter contrasts with austere cubes and steps leading to the gallery of the left-hand cube. Counter and steps create a situation rather like an urban square between high, two-storey structures – the trade fair stand becomes an architectural event.

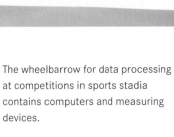

The wheelbarrow for data processing
at competitions in sports stadia
contains computers and measuring
devices.

Galvanized sheet-metal tables and stands.
IBM Telecom 1979 (page 221).

Furniture system for IBM Telecom 1987 (page 42).

The furniture system for IBM Telecom
1983 (page 227) echoes conceptual
characteristics of the stand container
(columns, surfaces).
It was used for years, and not only
at shows.

251

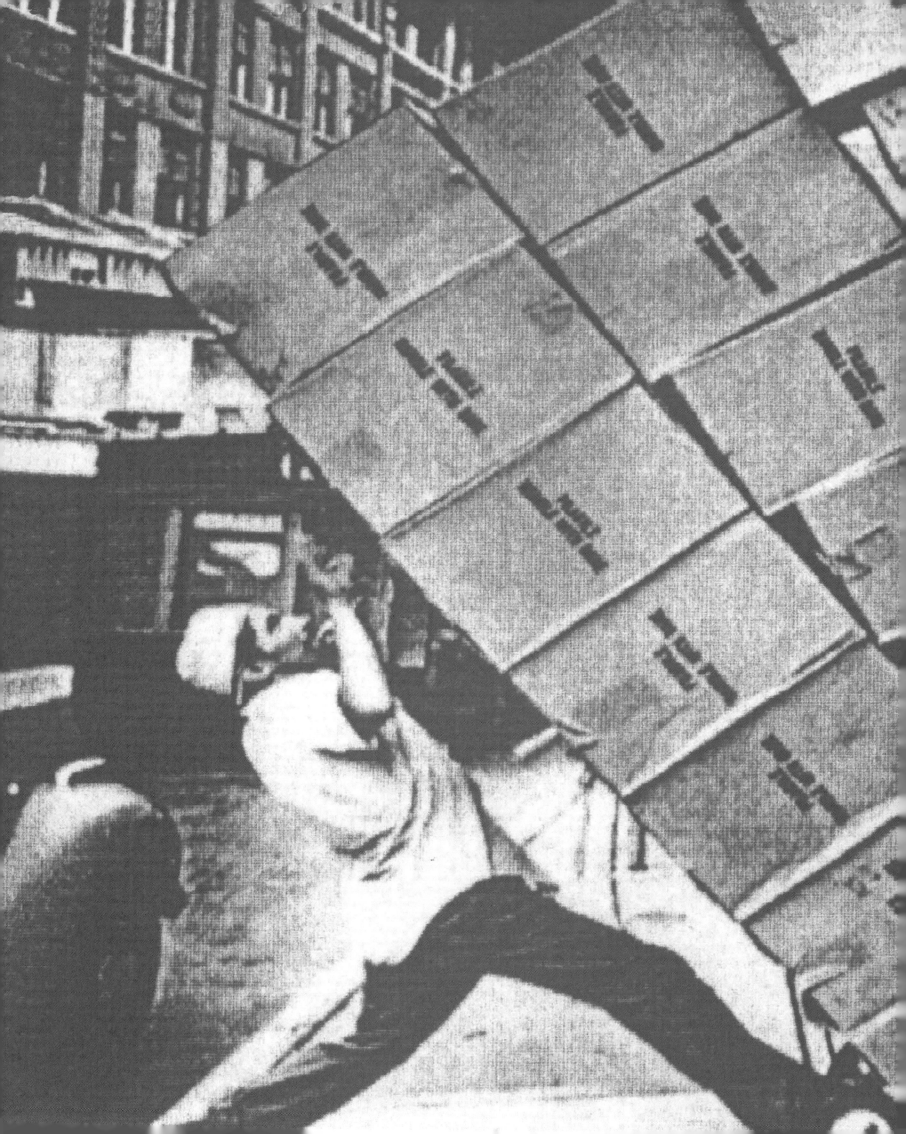

Working

Methods

Edgar Reinhard's firm consists of one person: Edgar Reinhard. He doesn't even have a secretary at his disposal. Nevertheless everything he does is highly professional. Why? Because Reinhard is just as talented an organizer as he is a designer. At every phase of a commission, from design via presentation, manufacture and logistics right down to documentation, he consults specialists. Professional draughtsmen and model-makers present the designs in visual form and provide him with the basis he needs to check his design work. Despite the advanced presentation technology available on computer, a technology he has completely mastered, traditional devices like hand-made perspectives or models remain of central importance.

Sometimes computer drawings are used as a basis for drawings by hand because the emotive quality of a designer's handwriting cannot be achieved by a computer image, which may be perfect but therefore sterile as well. And a model or prototype on the scale 1:1 provides more reliable insights than a two-dimensional computer image, which only allows as much freedom to observe as the programmer will allow.

Impressive as a 3-D presentation on the screen can be, there is also the danger of distortion. With a full-scale or detailed model, design qualities can be understood even by a layman – an important point, as the people who make the decisions are not builders or designers but managers. A model also helps in consultations with the subsequent manufacturers during the design phase. Problem points can be identified, checked and corrected at an early stage: the experts' suggestions become an integral part of the subsequent design process.

For example, Reinhard originally suggested using clad 'H' girders for the main lateral supports of the floating IBM pavilion. But then the steel erector suggested building a tube-stabilized triangular girder of thick sheet metal. This solution was not only technically simpler, but also more attractive visually, as the tubular components also structured the girders. Early consultation was also important here in terms of assembly and logistics. Thus, for example, the parts were dimensioned in such a way that no special transport was necessary. And reliability of assembly was also a priority for Reinhard since he would be faced with heavy fines for delays: three per cent of the building costs for every day's delay. Besides this, IBM had retained the right to use other firms to finish the pavilion in case of doubt.

Reinhard's reticent use of graphic materials is striking and goes against the trend. As a partner in Wirz Identity he has easy access to other subsidiaries of that firm who are concerned with corporate identity and graphic design. But this reticence is conditioned conceptually: consumer research has revealed that company slogans at trade fairs, for example, are often not connected with the correct firm afterwards – you risk advertising your competitors with your own slogan. So Reinhard used no slogans at all for the 1991 Telecom show – the IBM Networking lettering was simply placed in a prominent position.

Documenting what has been done is also part of the overall planning – if you don't think of it in time, all you have left of your work is the memory, and that is difficult to sell. For the Telecom show, Reinhard engaged a Swiss Television team at his own expense. The Toyota stand was also filmed professionally and the sound dubbed later in English by a Swiss Radio International broadcaster. Reinhard has pictorial presentation material recorded on video and CD – very easy to carry around and show to clients and journalists alike.

Reinhard works in a ruthlessly competitive field and large trade fair building firms often fight for each others' business by providing free concept suggestions. A small operation like Reinhard's can only hold its own if a client can be convinced of the quality of a project from the outset. So he offers worked-out concepts only when invited, and that involves a fee. Anyone who is concerned with a high level of creative quality in the field would do well to adopt the same procedure. It does absolutely no good for the esteem in which good design is held if it is just assumed to be a free pre-investment. A good project stems from the involvement of many specialists, and a concept for a competition that is just thrown together with the minimum effort often turns out to be a flop.

Even if a concept is impressive at the outset, it may have to be passed on from one team to another because the person who came up with the original idea does not know how to translate it into reality. Projects for small companies are sometimes planned too ambitiously and end up with the big trade fair building companies. This means that the designer loses control and recognizes only the vaguest outlines of his original idea in the end result. With one exception (Metallgesellschaft project, page 258), Reinhard has always been able to convince his clients of the advantages of one person as designer-organizer. The commercial attraction is that the risk is better with a designer-producer compared with offering services simply as a designer, and this is the financial basis of a one-man business of this kind.

A theatrical arrangement.

**Metallgesellschaft
Hanover 1986, project**

This is a symbolic representation of an iron-ore mine. The arena-like arrangement presents a hierarchy of the individual show places and imparts enhanced significance – 'cultural charging'. Today the process of iron-smelting and metal exploitation tends to be a pragmatic one, and here it is short-circuited, as it were, by the theatrical arrangement with prehistoric motifs.

Significance is borrowed from a time when the blacksmith was at the centre of small communities and was endowed with almost magical attributes of power. The archaic gate sculptures are reminiscent of contemporary concrete art by Max Bill, and also of common cultural property like Stonehenge or South American temples with their stepped structures. The four most important metals for this company, which operates with raw materials, are joined in a knot inside the building.

The professional sketch is an effective tool for emotive visual presentation. These drawings were created from the background of computer-generated stereometric designs.

As the built stand did not conform to the designer's ideas, a model photograph is used for the illustration here.

A perfect model creates more trust than a perfect on-screen presentation. You can touch it and look at it from all angles. It is a tangible reality, and that is important when managers have to be persuaded.

This presentation plays with iconographic associations: Stonehenge, amphitheatre, temple. These are images that everyone knows. The mythological charge emanating from this raw process suggests that the enterprise is very

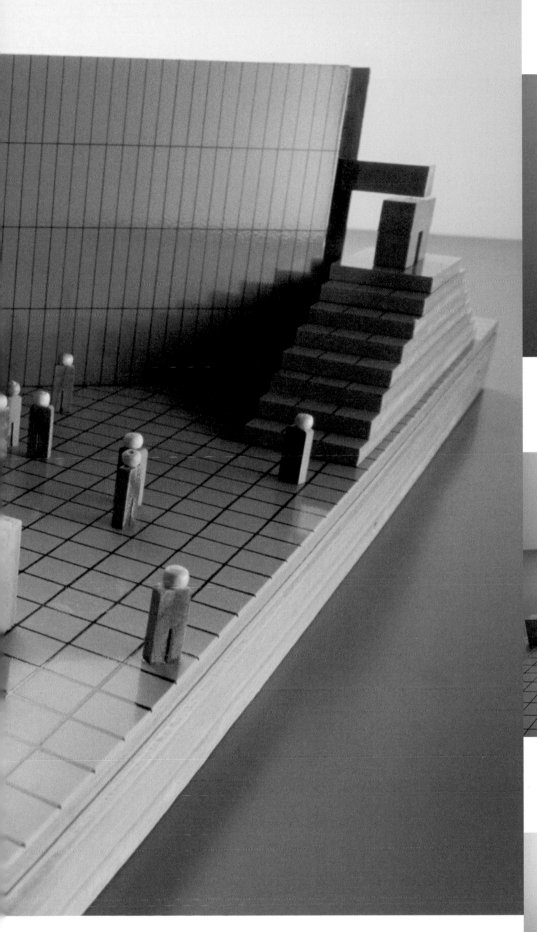

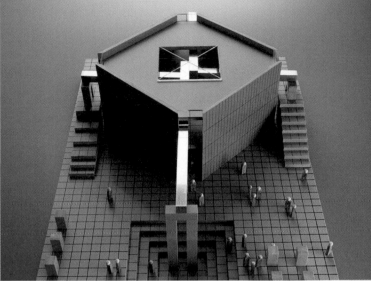

significant, but it makes very heavy demands
in terms of the materials used for realization
if the whole thing is not to degenerate into first-
rate kitsch.

The suspended office.

Karl Steiner
Zurich 1990, project

Steiner AG is one of the largest building and property companies in Switzerland. The office complex is suspended on piers above an existing building in the Oerlikon district of Zurich. This meant that expensive demolition and remodelling work could be avoided. The project won first prize in the competition but was not executed because of the building slump. (Engineering: Urs Schneider, Schneider Stahlbau AG, Jona)

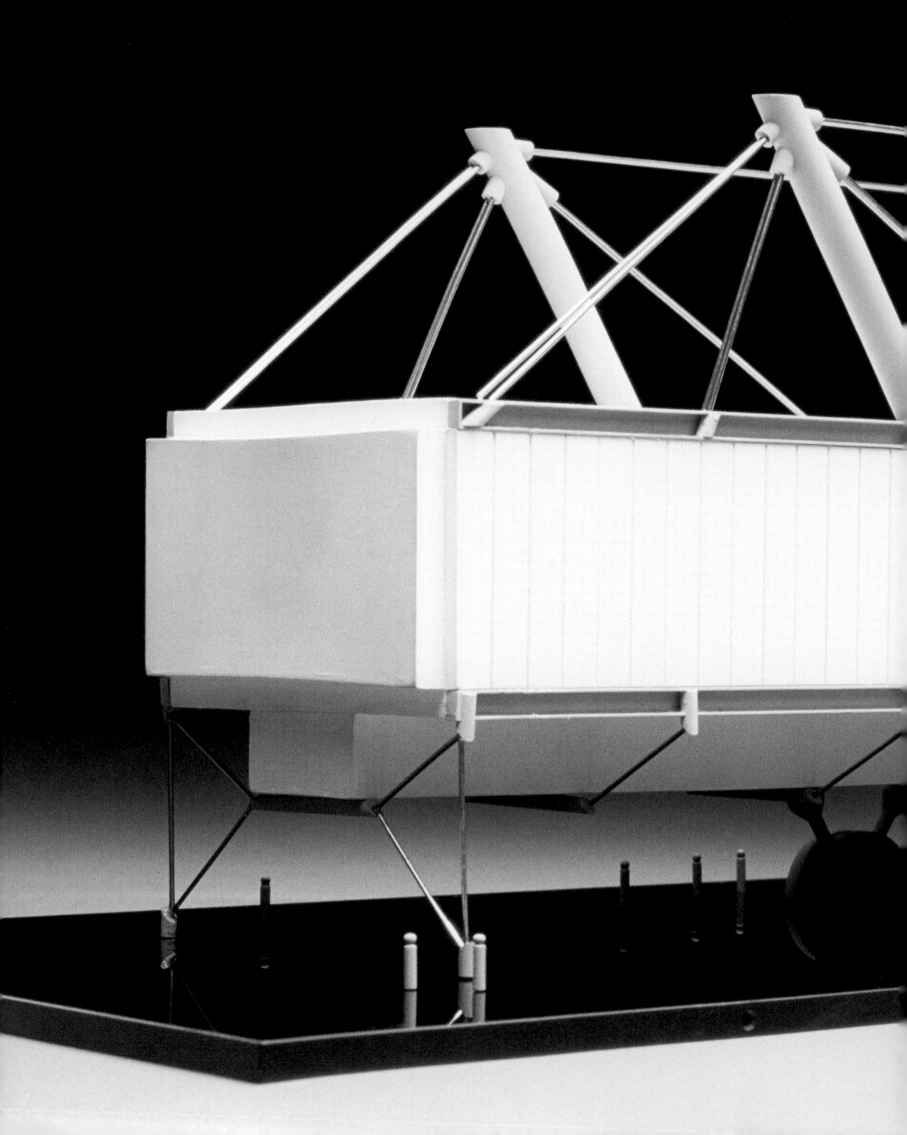

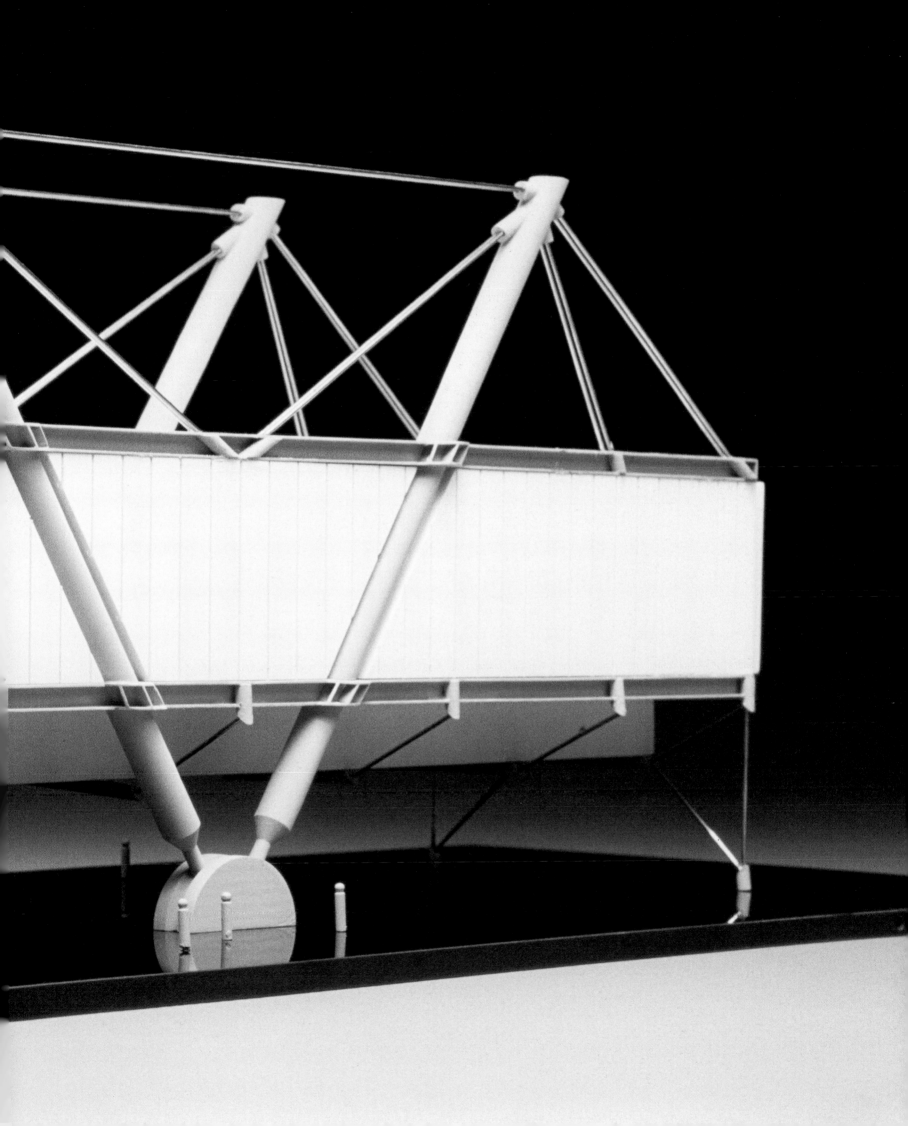

Do the unexpected to give visitors an impression they will not forget.

General Motors, Opel
1995, project

Reinhard wrote this sentence on the dossier for his competition entry for Opel's new image for international Motor shows. Here are the most important statements it contained:

'Objective
To develop a design which can not escape from the memory of the visitors and not be imitated by competitors. Also the average consumer must be able to understand and interpret the message.
Competitive Environment
Motor Shows are dominated by large stands of high design quality and creativity.
All actual design trends are already represented.

Options
Consequently Opel has two options:
1. Avant-garde design
2. Unconventional solution that does not orientate itself towards any of the trends in vogue.
As an avant-garde solution will be hardly understood and appreciated by the majority of our target audience, we recommend opting for the second approach.'

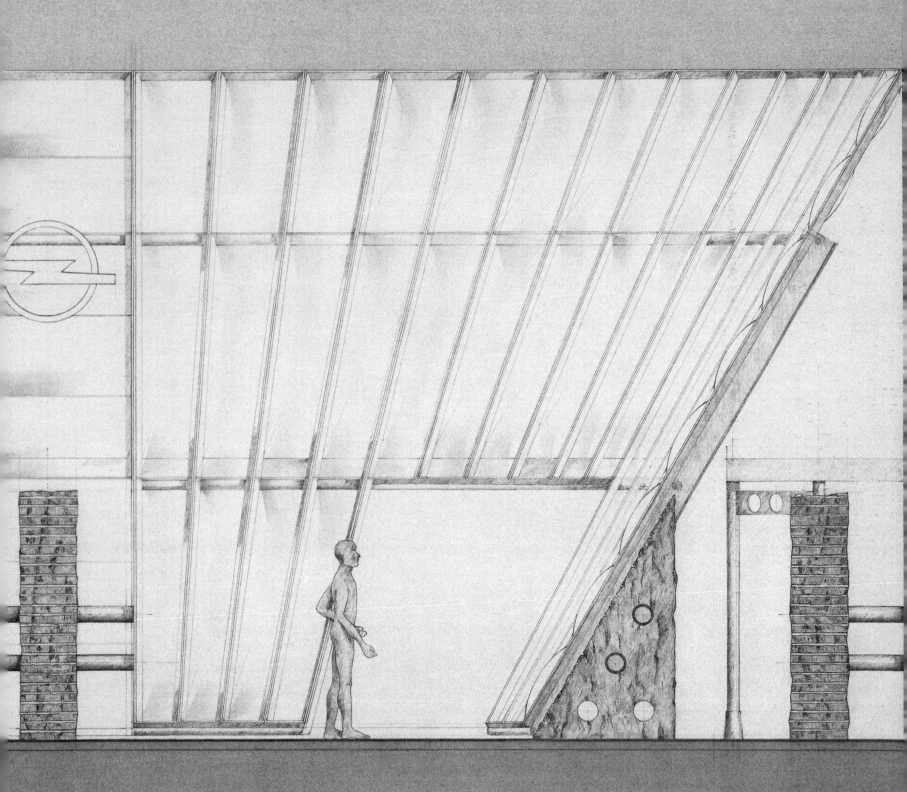

The scale model shows one of many possible layout solutions.
The distances between the structural elements of the stand even allow
for the passing of a safety corridor when required.

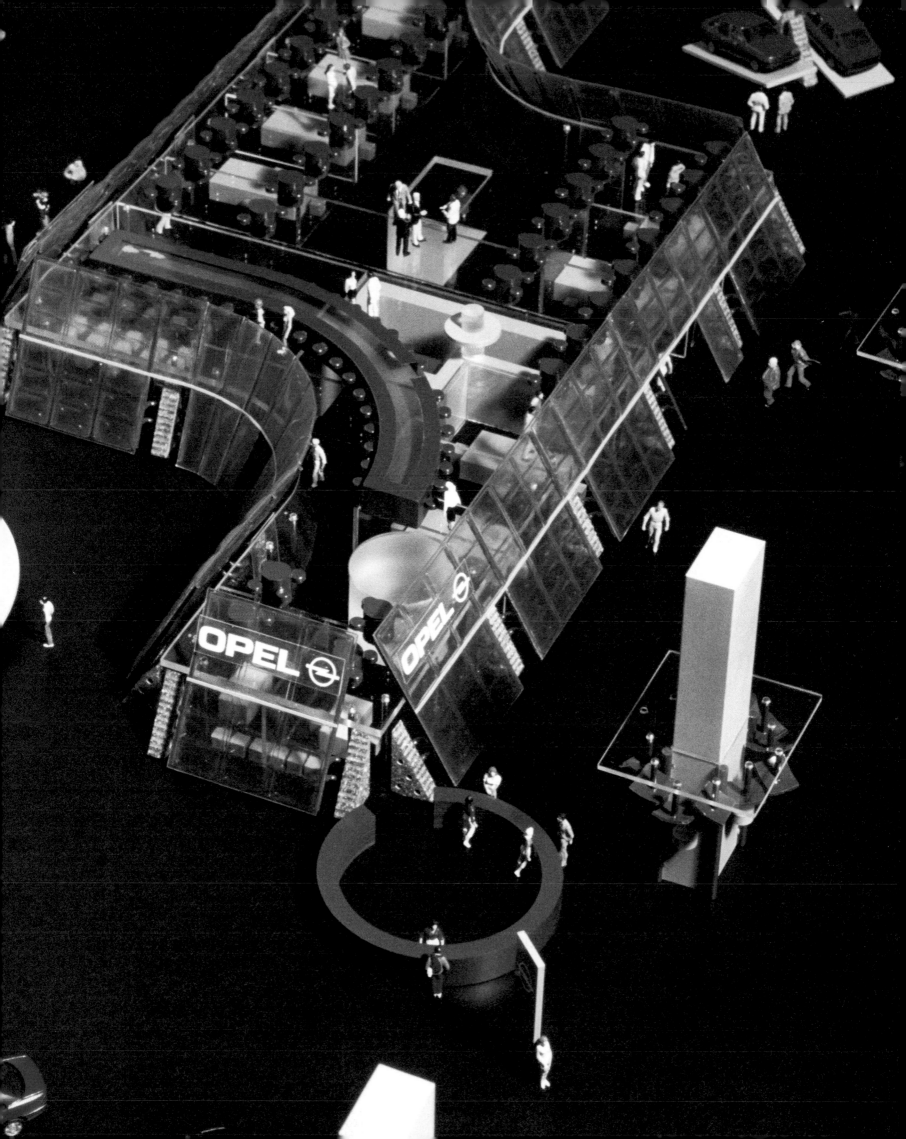

layout variations

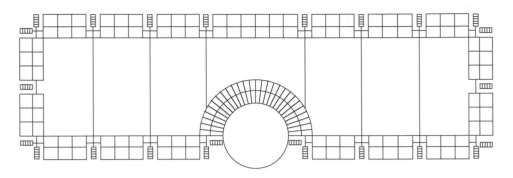

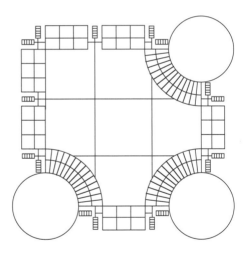

scale 1 : 500

Construction requirements

'Short construction and dismantling time. Modular design due to variety of space and construction heights available in different exhibitions (as demanded by organizer). Flexibility to adapt design and layout to the changing marketing requirements. Limited number of construction components (but allowing for great number of design variations). Structure designed to compensate for differences in dimensional tolerance of stone elements.'

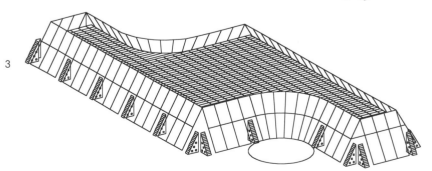

1 Placing stones
2 Putting on the floor/ceiling system
3 Fitting the inflatable cladding
   elements ('airbags')

section

front view

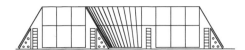

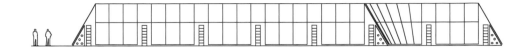

floor plan

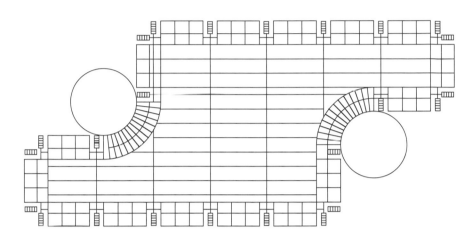

scale 1 : 500

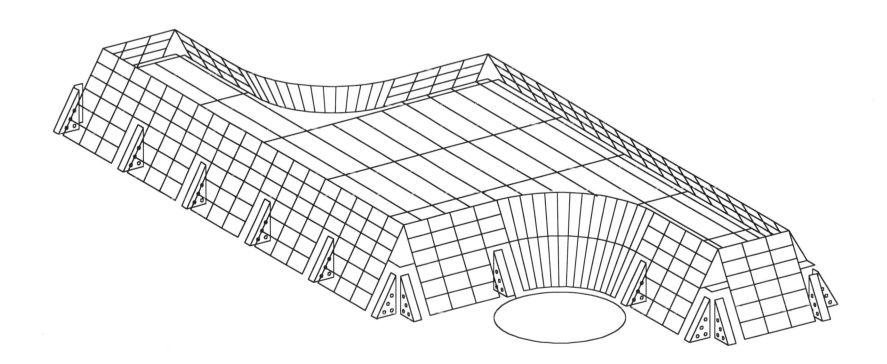

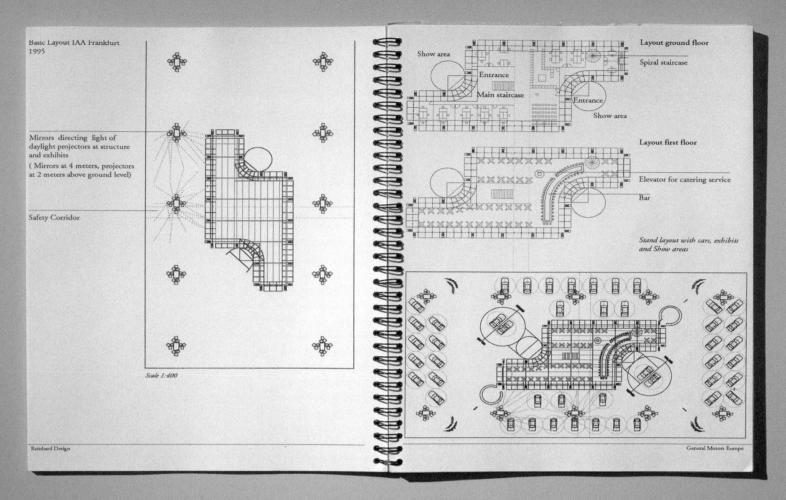

Basic Layout IAA Frankfurt
1995

Mirrors directing light of
daylight projectors at structure
and exhibits
(Mirrors at 4 meters, projectors
at 2 meters above ground level)

Safety Corridor

Scale 1:400

Reinhard Design

Show area

Entrance

Main staircase

Entrance

Show area

Layout ground floor

Spiral staircase

Layout first floor

Elevator for catering service

Bar

*Stand layout with cars, exhibits
and Show areas*

General Motors Europe

After the model, project documentation is the most important device for convincing customers.

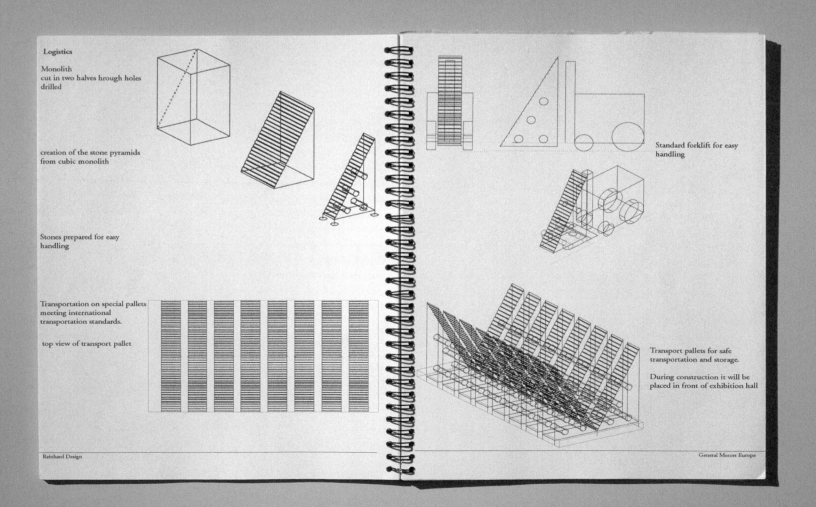

Logistics

Monolith
cut in two halves through holes
drilled

creation of the stone pyramids
from cubic monolith

Stones prepared for easy
handling

Transportation on special pallets
meeting international
transportation standards.

top view of transport pallet

Reinhard Design

Standard forklift for easy
handling

Transport pallets for safe
transportation and storage.

During construction it will be
placed in front of exhibition hall

General Motors Europe

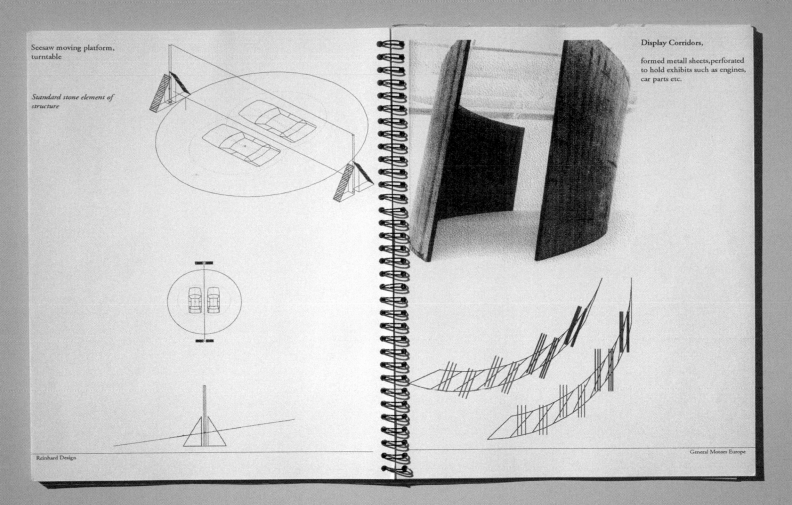

Seesaw moving platform, turntable

Standard stone element of structure

Display Corridors,

formed metall sheets, perforated to hold exhibits such as engines, car parts etc.

Reinhard Design

General Motors Europe

Reinhard's documentation of the Opel competition project was a fifty-page brochure, from which four double pages are printed here.

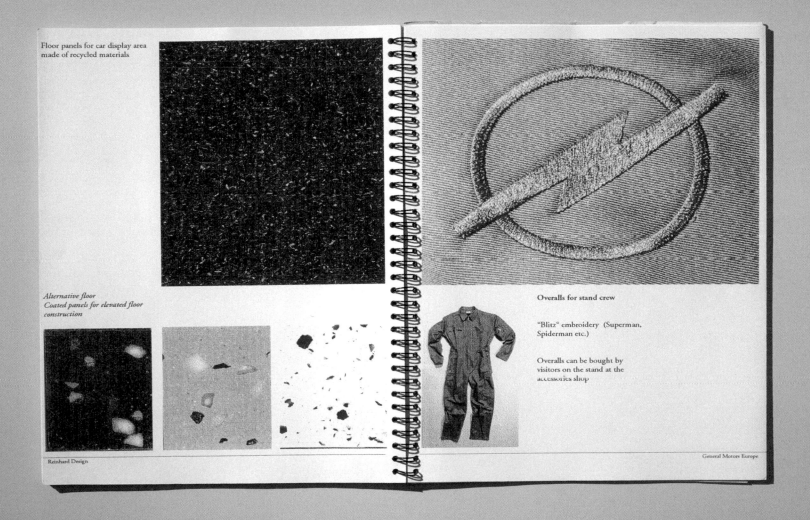

Floor panels for car display area made of recycled materials

Alternative floor
Coated panels for elevated floor construction

Overalls for stand crew

"Blitz" embroidery (Superman, Spiderman etc.)

Overalls can be bought by visitors on the stand at the accessories shop

Reinhard Design

General Motors Europe

'Creative Recycling'
In Poll Position for the conquest of the markets
of the future.

IBM
World Exhibition of Telecommunications
Geneva 1991

Although Reinhard had already dealt with several projects for Telecom, the client always requested a new concept for each new appearance, as part of a competition presentation. As the floating pavilion had proved its worth in 1987, the modified project was accepted on two further occasions. Even so, a great deal of persuasion was still needed with drawings, plans, calculations and models.

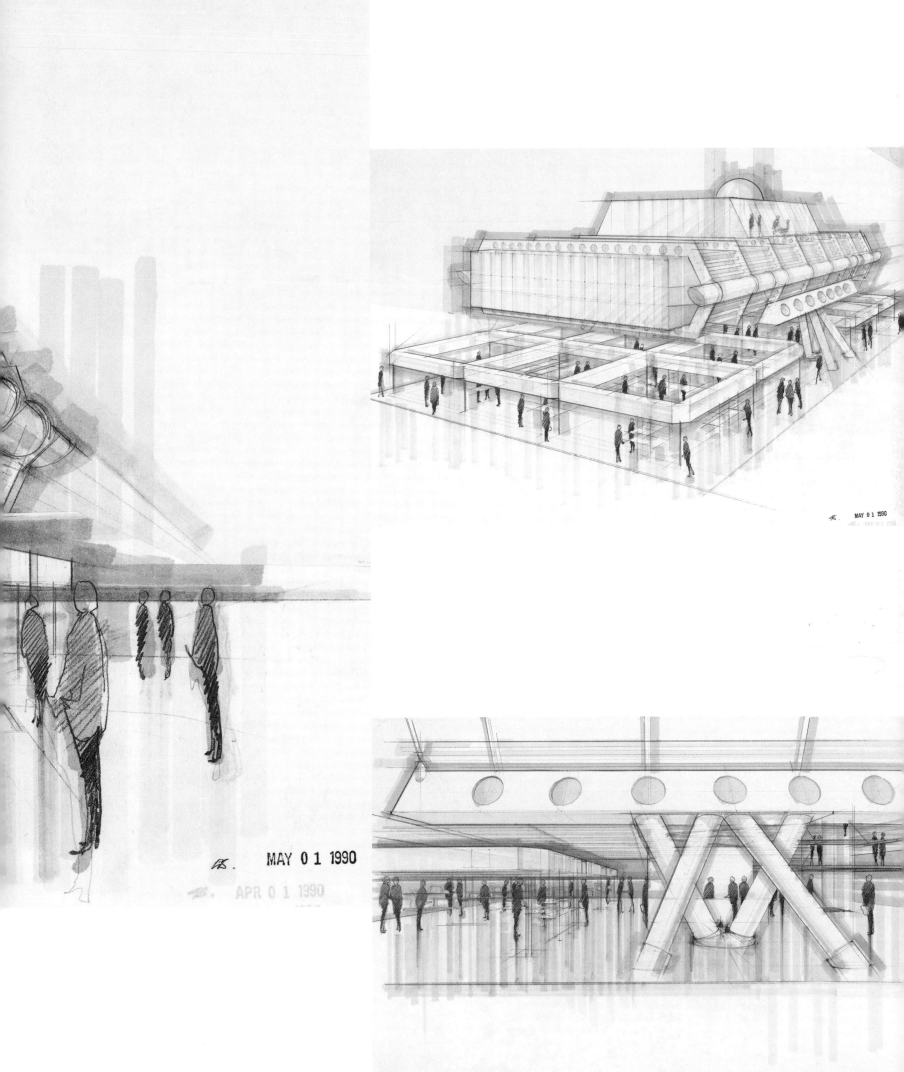

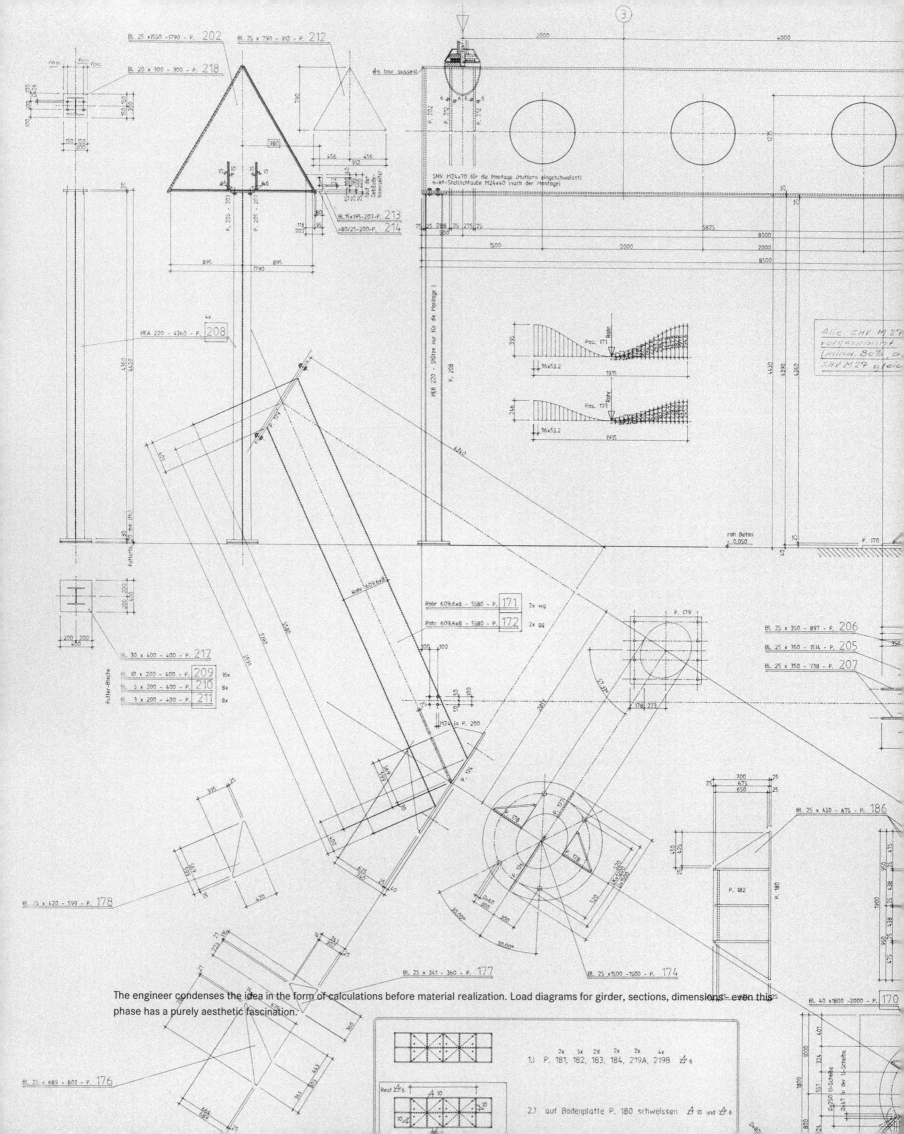

The engineer condenses the idea in the form of calculations before material realization. Load diagrams for girder, sections, dimensions — even this phase has a purely aesthetic fascination.

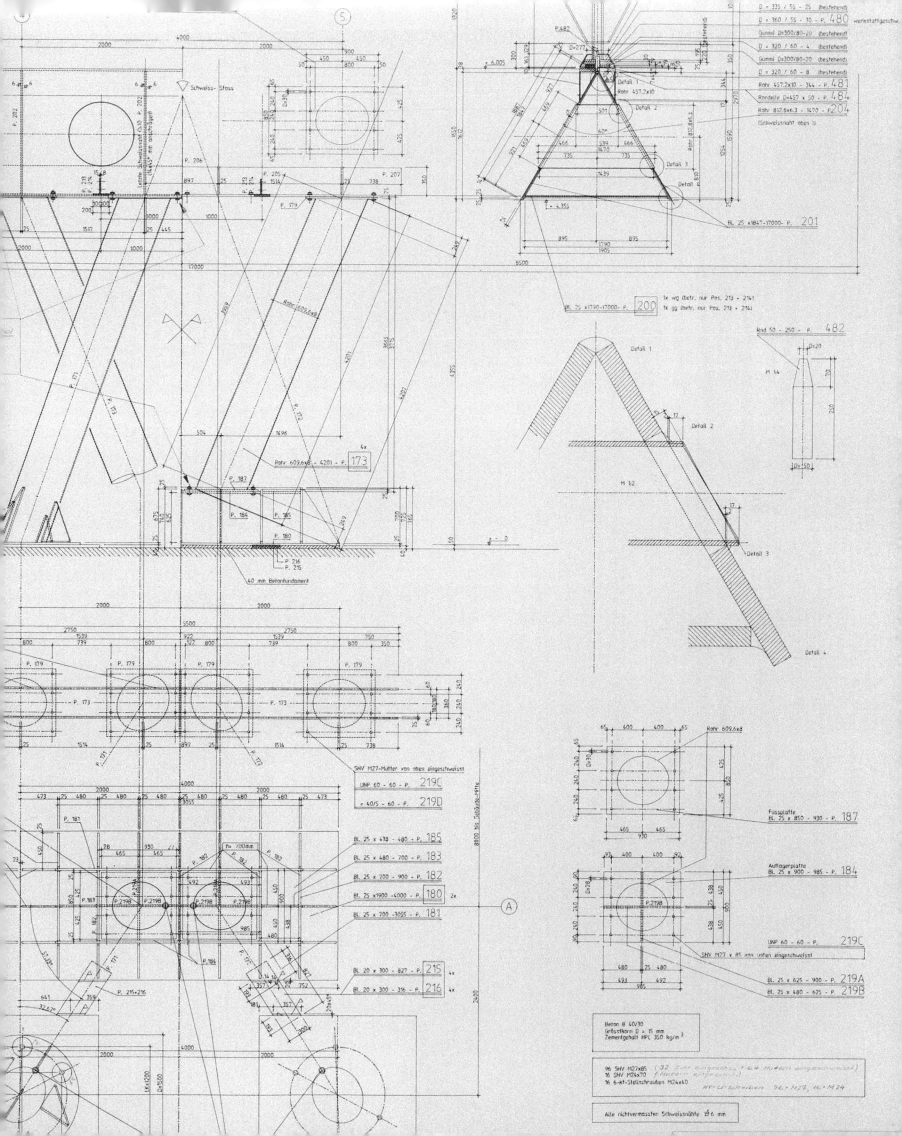

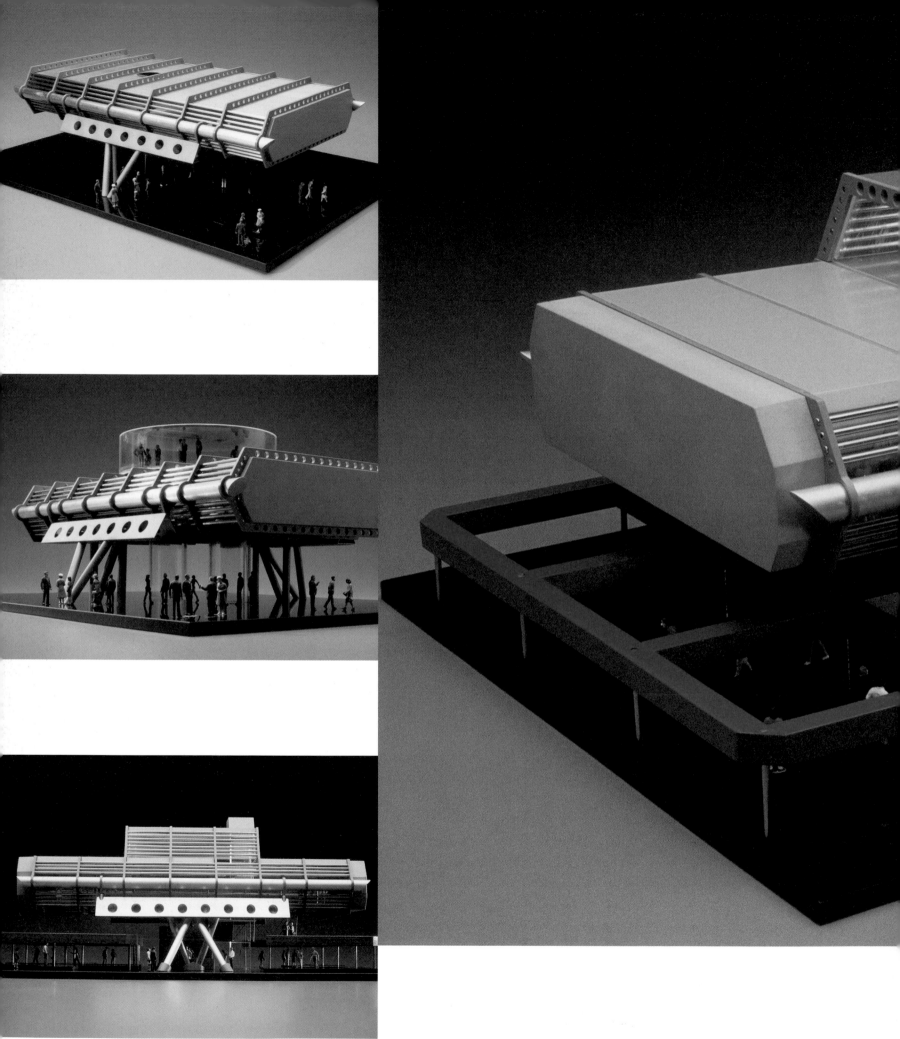

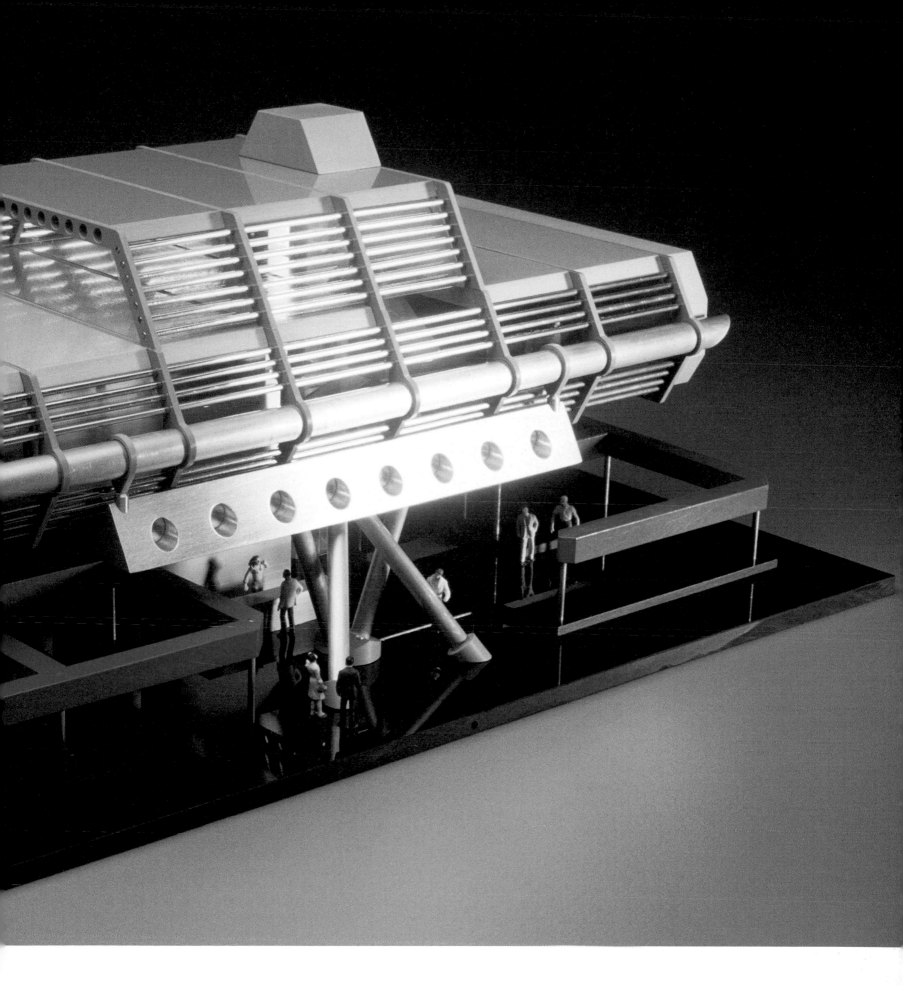

Reinhard invested tens of thousands of dollars in the models for the IBM pavilions. Every appearance by the Shuttle had to be fought for with IBM – and models played a part every time. They are an endless source of fascination to visitors to the studio – small, passionate objects protected by their glass case. The 1991 model is illustrated.

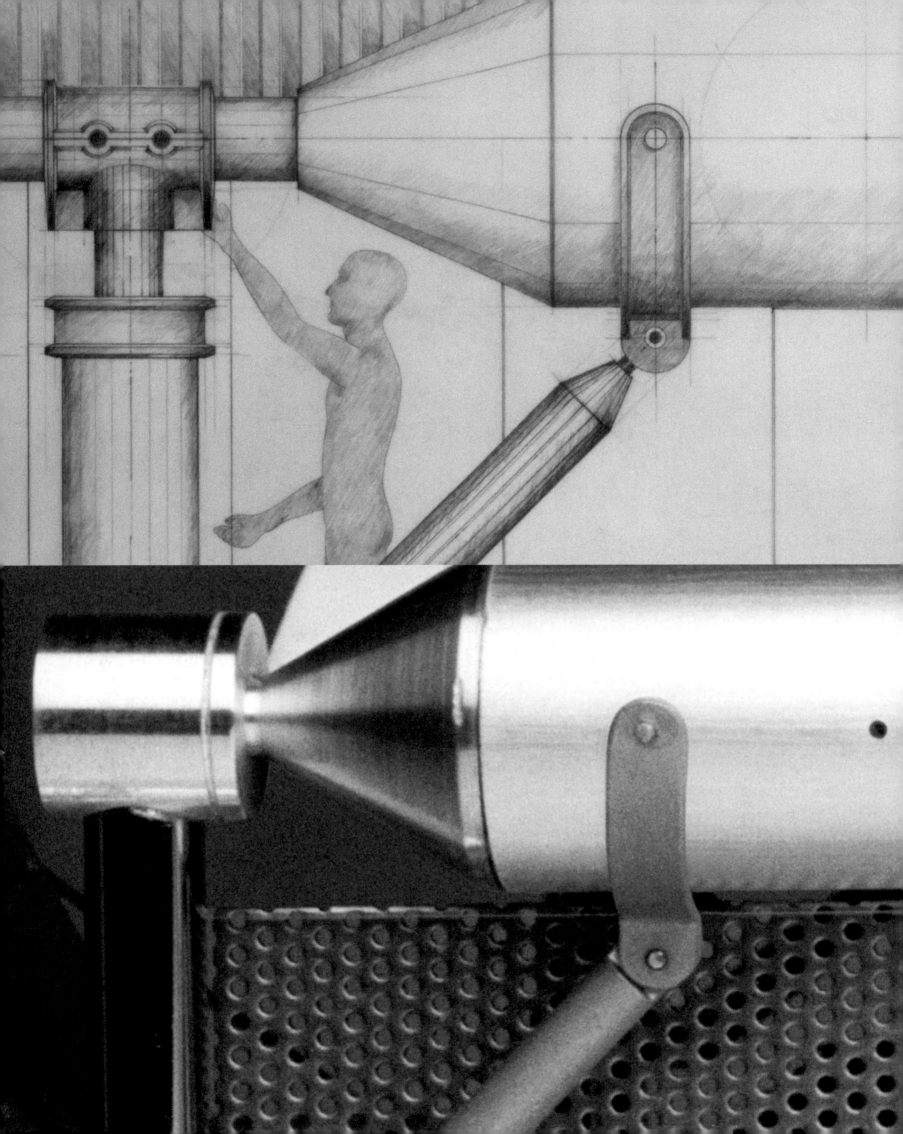

Leadership in technology must be reflected in the stand design.

Toyota
European Motor Shows
1990

When submitting the project in 1989, Edgar Reinhard put forward the following consideration:
'BMW and Mercedes exhibition stands can hardly be beaten in terms of design perfection and execution. Visitors have grown accustomed to this 'deluxe' standard which uses stainless steel, granite, marble and extravagant audio-visual and display techniques – they hardly find it exceptional anymore. One thing is common to all Toyota cars and important to all Toyota clients: the favourable relationship between price and performance. This is of particular significance because Toyota customers represent a wide range of people with varying purchasing power and taste.
So, what can be done to draw attention to the corporate philosophy with the help of visual, architectural, design and construction engineering means? Toyota's leadership in technology must be reflected by the stand design. This approach will be more effective than the "me too" competition in the fashionable furnishing of the stands.'

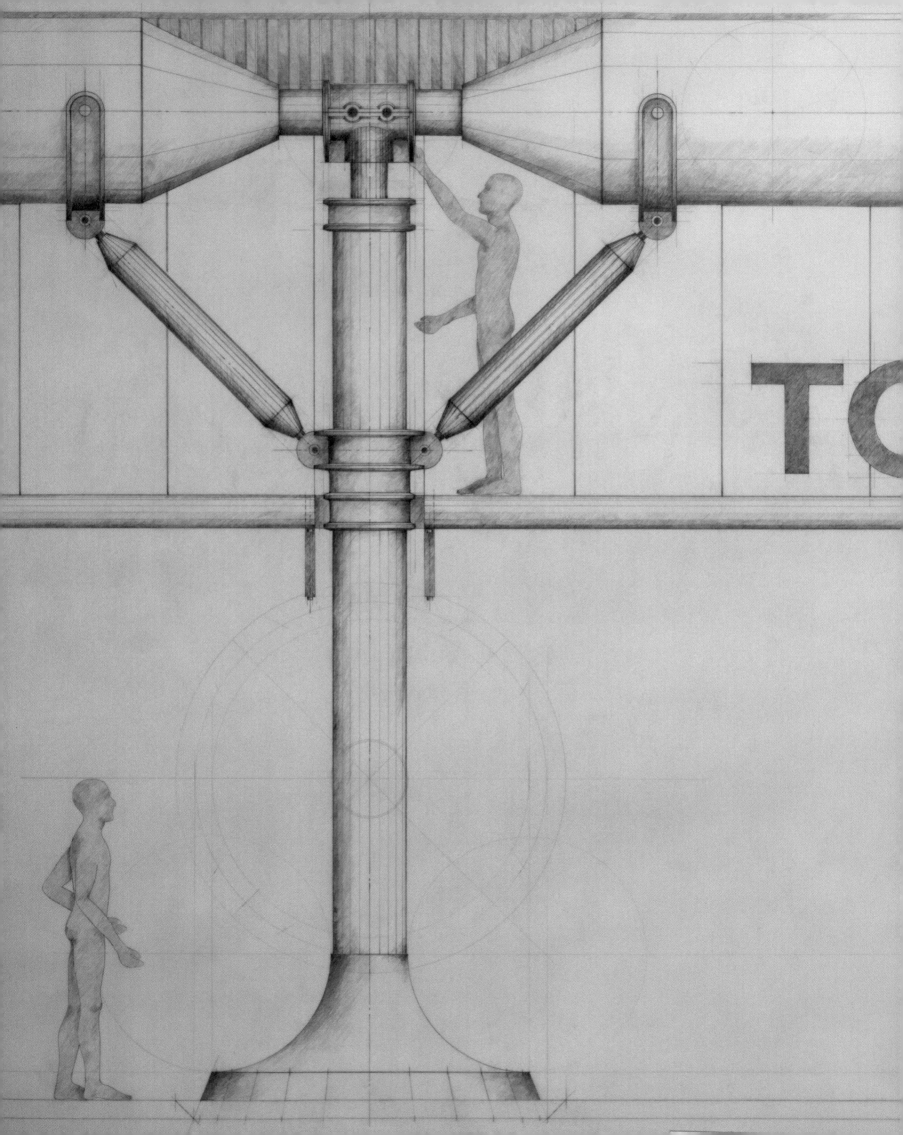

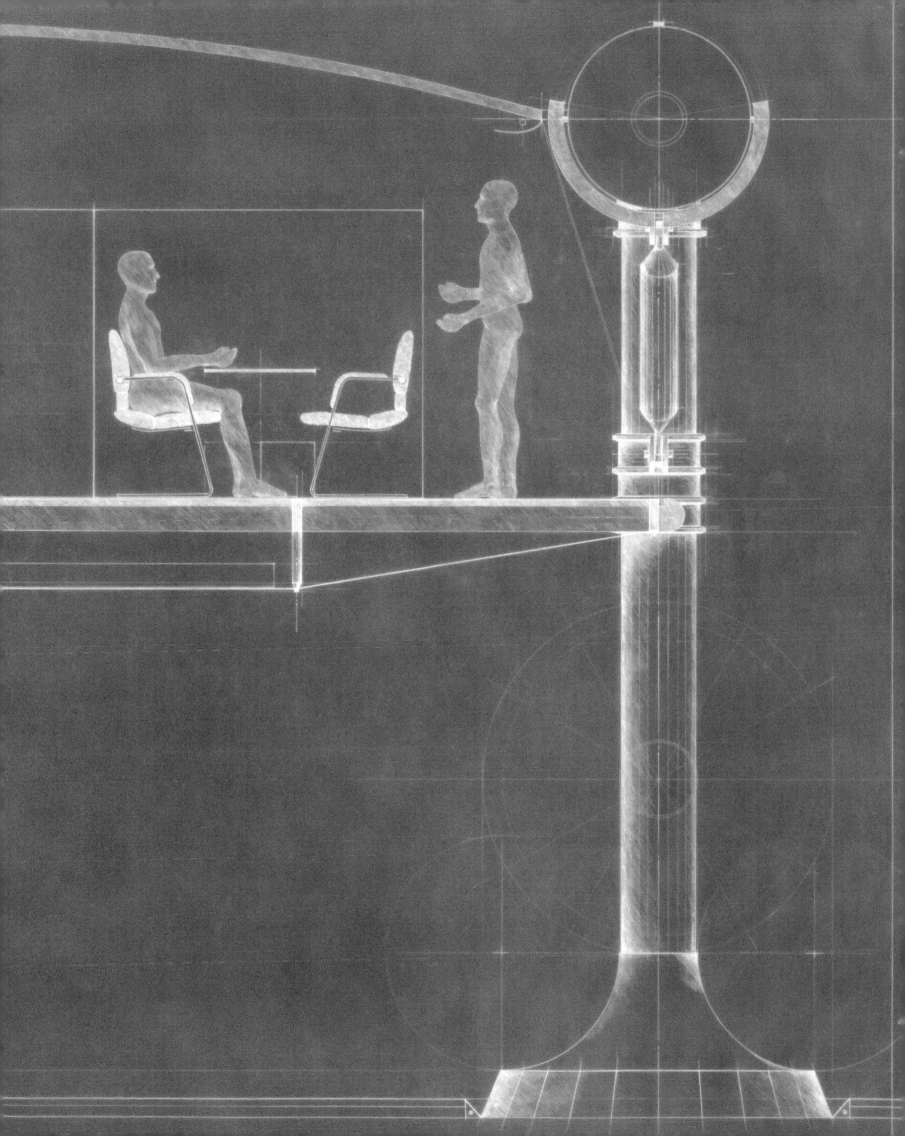

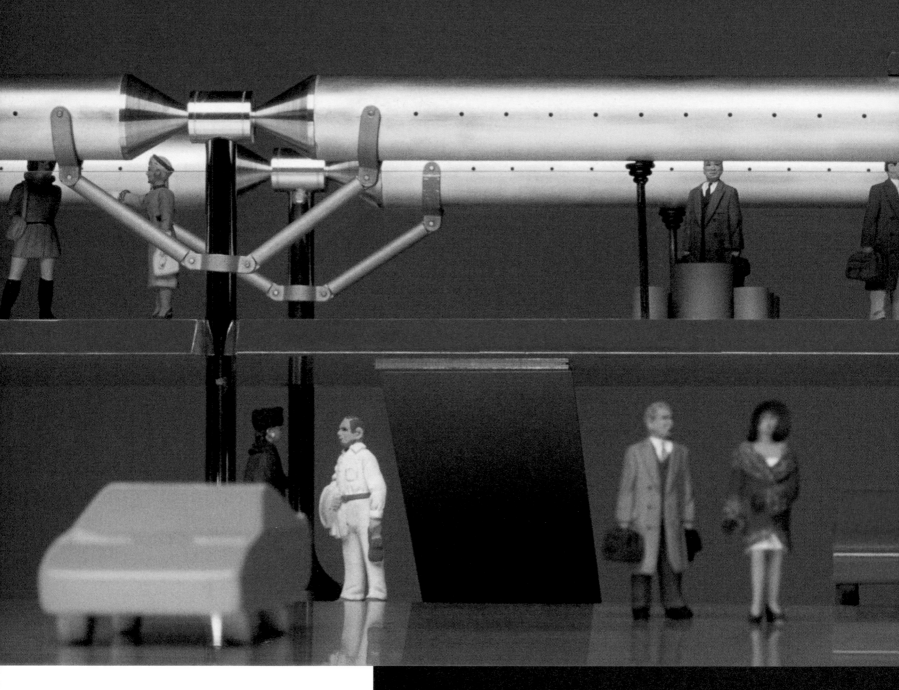

The original concept provided for a crane
between the main supports to make assembly
easier.

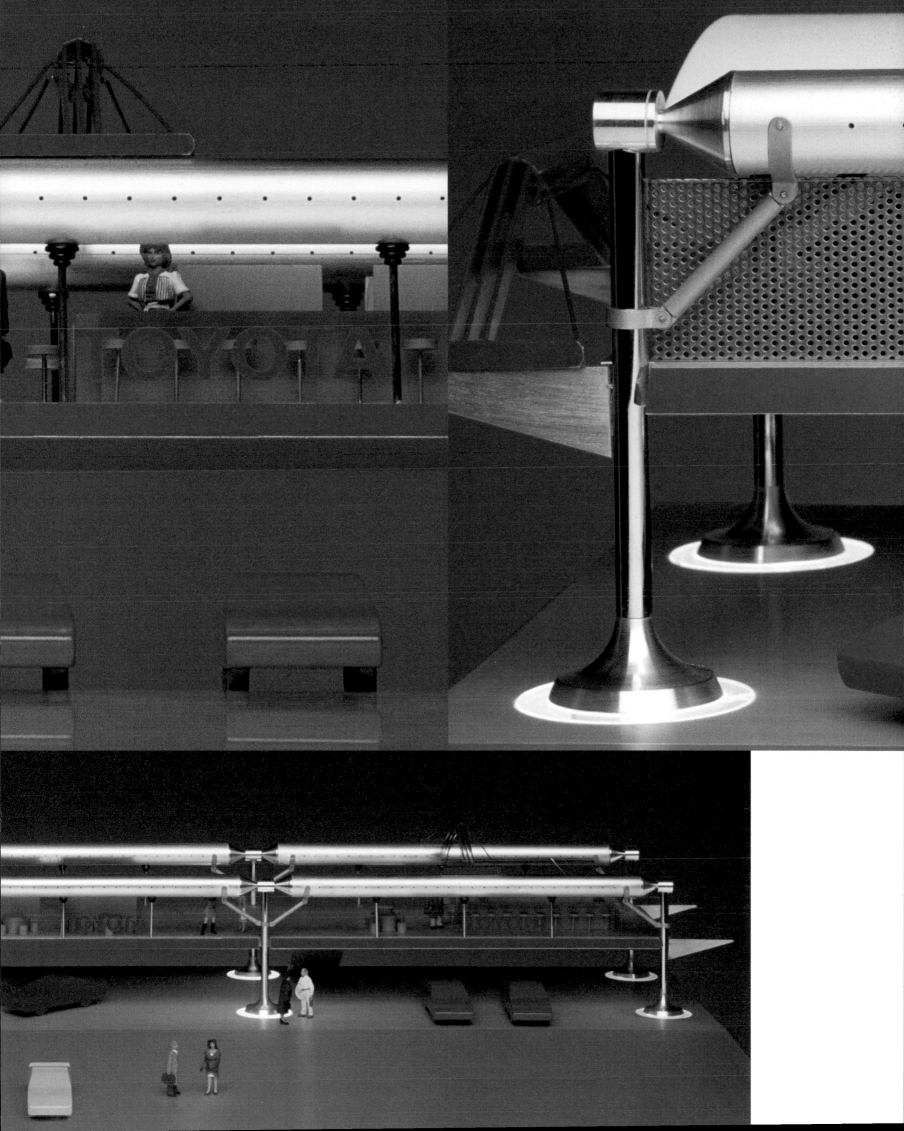

Edgar Reinhard

Anyone who knows Edgar Reinhard's work and then gets to know the man behind it is surprised at first: Is it possible that such large projects can be planned and realized from this studio? Anyone expecting a staff of draughtsmen and technicians will be disappointed. Edgar Reinhard works alone in this refuge on the edge of a wood with pool and romantic garden near Zurich. He has no employees. Until it was modified recently the Gockhausen studio was both his home and his workplace. By the open fire stands a tower of electronic equipment. Shelves of books and models, plans and sketches wherever you look make the spacious room more like a cave occupied by a person possessed, who lives with his work. Reinhard talks about his work reticently, shows videos first of all and only gradually starts to talk, searches for words to explain something that he produces almost automatically, as if it could not possibly be different. But behind this reticence the clarity of his thought that can be seen in his work soon shines through the conversation. He once said in an interview that he works with customers who know what they want.

Edgar Reinhard learned from practice, rather than theory. He does not follow established concepts like Bauhaus, Deconstructivism or post-Modernism, but mentions the personalities who shaped his development. Josef Müller-Brockmann, the internationally known Swiss graphic designer, and Paul Gredinger, the co-founder of a large advertising agency as an opposite personality, were direct influences on Reinhard. Another guiding light was the world-famous graphic designer Paul Rand, who created logos for IBM, Next and Westinghouse.

Reinhard's unconventional path from training as a lithographer and then as a graphic designer to become a self-taught designer of exhibition stands left him free to avoid having to shake off the doctrines of architecture, advertising or design. His work cannot be precisely classified because, as we have already established, it represents something unique, a discipline in its own right. His origins are in advertising as much as design. He describes himself as a 'three-dimensional advertiser', thus stressing that the advertising impact of trade fair stands is not rated highly enough in his opinion. It is typical that his only professional partnership is with an advertising firm and not with a designer: Reinhard is a partner in the Zurich Agency Wirz Identity, which handles three-dimensional advertising design.

Meeting establishes trust. Reinhard feels that the possibility of meeting face to face, the opportunity of meeting decision-makers from all over the world within a brief period, is not rated highly enough. Trade fair exhibition design is concerned primarily with advertising, not with designing space, even though there is no doubt that design quality makes a major contribution to success.

Someone who has followed Edgar Reinhard's work for decades and has also been involved in it as a partner is Hans Ulrich Schweizer, co-owner of the Wirz communications group and chairman of Wirz Identity in Zurich.

Edgar Reinhard and I came across each other for the first time in the late sixties. Reinhard was a young graphic artist and designer and approached me as creative director of Wirz to find out how to become an art director in an advertising agency. A glance at his portfolio was enough to show me that some sort of career as a director would not be enough for an extra-ordinary talent like Reinhard's. A radical young designer whose work is uncompromising in its quality should not choose a working environment where concessions become a question of survival.

So Edgar Reinhard went his own way. He listened to nothing but his own inner voice, and remained a radical thinker and a consistent and uncom-promising designer who made heavy demands on himself and his work. He reminds me of the Zen-Buddhist sculptor who, when asked why he always chiselled such beautiful lions out of the stone, is said to have answered that he just chipped off everything that did not look like lion.

My first encounter with Edgar Reinhard was the start of a close relation-ship running through our two careers. Many joint and prize-winning projects have been created by him and our advertising agency, and I am pleased today that Edgar Reinhard founded Wirz Identity AG with me in 1991; it became one of the leading Swiss Corporate Identity firms as little as three years later.

Hans Ulrich Schweizer

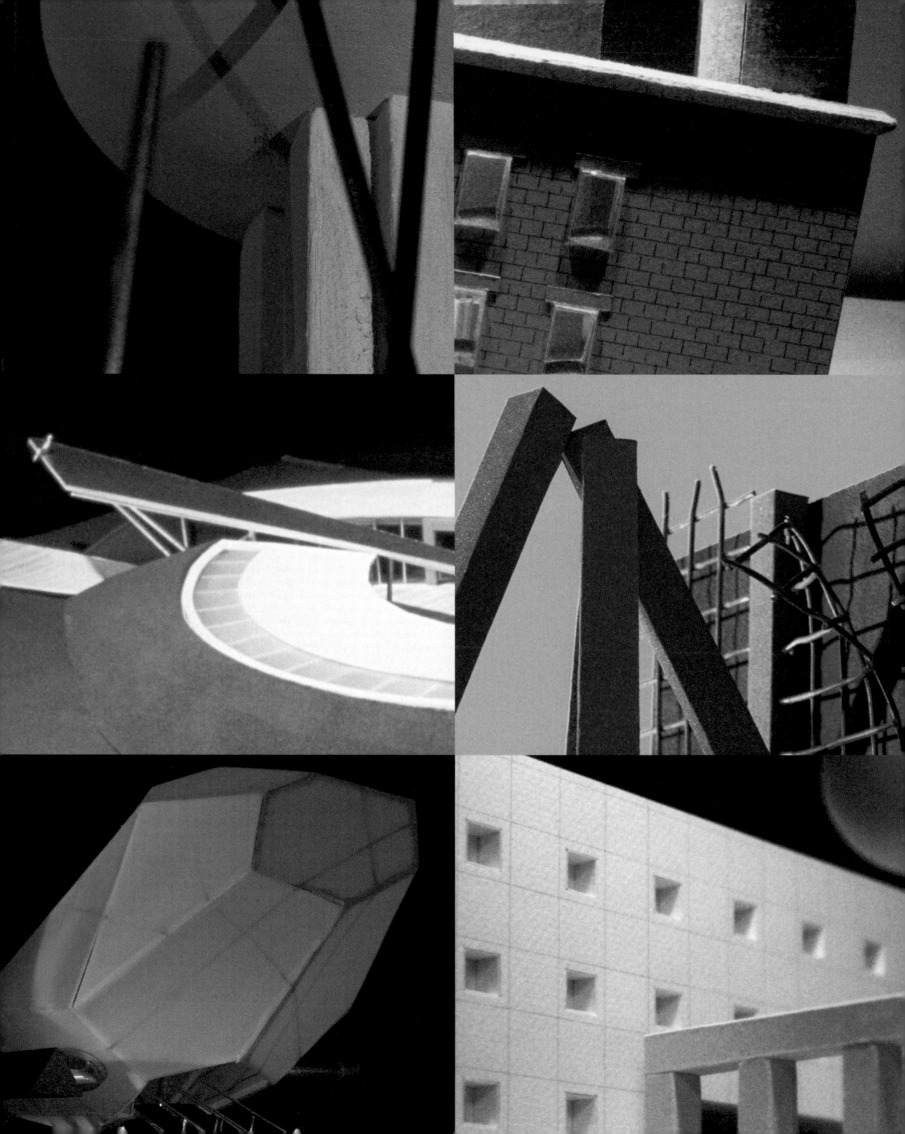

The Teacher

Edgar Reinhard is professor at the Lippe Fachhochschule in Detmold (North-Rhine Westphalia, Germany), and attracts large numbers of students, probably because he does not take an academic line, but tries to adapt his own career within the educational context and to pass it on in this way. The problems he sets arise from practice, and where possible the task relates to a real requirement. For example, his students entered a competition for a stand for the steel manufacturer Mannesmann. Reinhard recommended that they should not stick to the requirements laid down by the firm, but define the best possible conditions themselves. The result proved him right: one of the students' suggestion for a mobile, strongly abstract presentation with some of the characteristics of an installation, presented on CD, won second prize. Another practice exercise was to design something completely new using the support structure from the IBM Shuttle stand. (Reinhard had acquired the supports and the steel skeleton after they were used for the last time in 1995.)

Plurality not uniformity
The diversity of the suggestions presented is staggering. Another realistic project was to design a pavilion for Switzerland as guest of honour at the 1998 Frankfurt Book Fair. Twenty-six projects, with a wide range of different approaches, were presented by the students, including a large number of women. The most important thing is not that one of the projects, or an idea from it, was executed, but that the students were working on something close to reality. Unfortunately the realization phase cannot be simulated. Preparing for it is the highest aim of Reinhard's very individual teaching.

Teaching guidelines and students' works

Designing exhibition stands is first of all a question of effective communication, and only secondly a question of style or formal decisions.

Concepts have to be based on ideas about content, not on design habits or fashionable topicality.

An exhibition stand is not a detached art object, but an integrating element of Corporate Design or Corporate Identity.

Organization is an important part of the whole; a design solution that does not work is not a solution.

In this sphere, as in many others, there is no success without risk.

The designer has to convince the client about this.
But not just the client.
Everyone who works on a project must be convinced by it.

Stand design has to be unique and impossible to imitate.

A high quality design concept also motivates everyone involved: the client, employees, customers and of course planners and others involved in the contract as well.
It is only by pulling together that extraordinary exhibition stands can be designed that attract and motivate visitors.

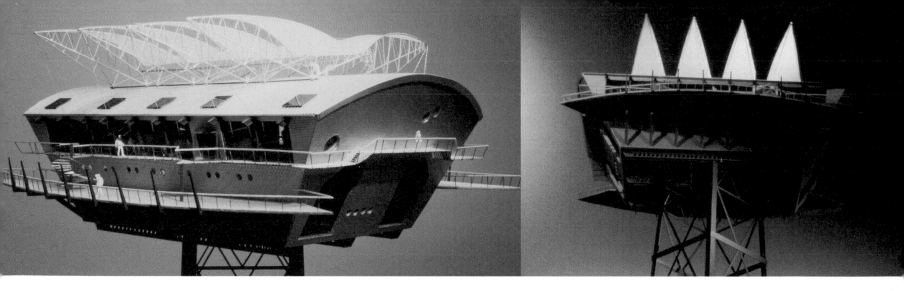

Stop for a cable railway in Barcelona. The tower for the middle station was already fixed. A diploma project by Astrid Wolff and Carsten Croes.

'Built light' exhibition of students projects in the Deutsches Architekturzentrum in Berlin and in the Lichtforum of Zumtobel Staff in Lemgo.
A project by Dirk Bachmann, Frank Horlitz and Lars Möller.

Reinhard has acquired the main construction parts of the former IBM Telecom exhibition. It therefore made sense when he got his Lippe college students in Detmold (Germany) to devise new concepts on the basis of this support construction.

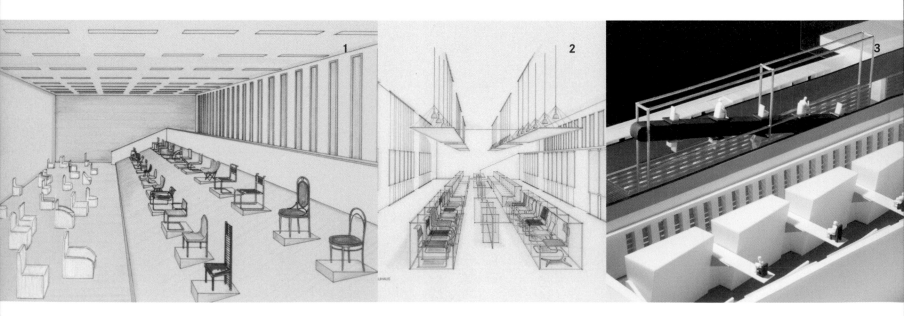

The Landesmuseum in Lippe was showing chairs from the Thonet collection. The students' suggestions included the ideas:
Who am I ? – the chair puzzle with concealed classics, the chair conveyor belt, Healthy Sitting as a theme using the row of stands as a spinal column or Gerrit Rietfeld's

From the volume and its changing coloured lighting to the pulsating body of the building – the students came up with some surprisingly independent solutions.

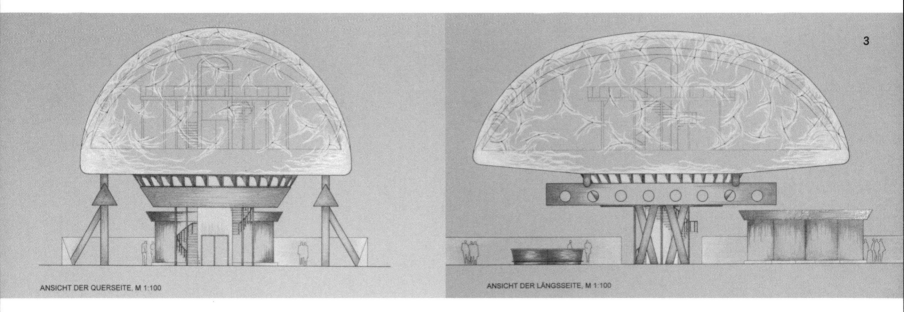

ANSICHT DER QUERSEITE, M 1:100

ANSICHT DER LÄNGSSEITE, M 1:100

1. Sybille Vogt, Andreas Frömel 2. Stefanie Bühlen, Torsten Busch 3. Andrea Mohme, Kerstin Steinert

chair icon as equipment for pedalos used on urban canals.
1. Michaela Strunk 2.Nicola Sigl 3. Stefanie Bühlen 4. Mirke Sellner, Eva Herrmann 5. Torsten Reuter, Klaus Kühlmann, Jens Birkholz

Reinhard realized four stands for Zürcher Ziegeleien, but the work shown on this page shows that the ideas were by no means exhausted. Admittedly many of these student concepts incline somewhat strongly to theatrical effect or alter things that are already familiar in their own way.

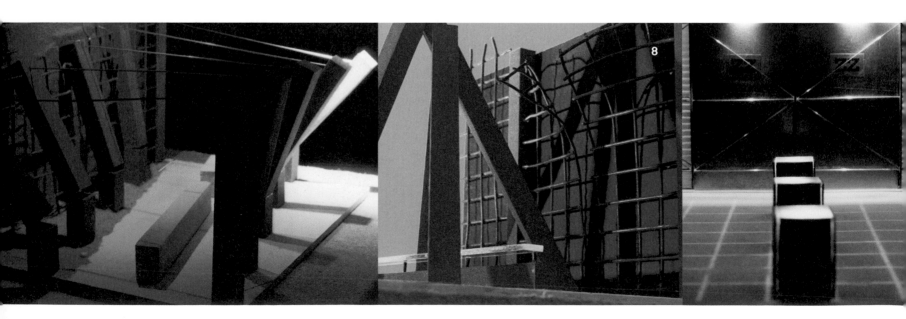

Even so, in some of the designs creative personalities can be seen to be emerging whose carefree approach must have been focused on specific requirements from a very early stage. How do I sell my idea? is also a constant theme that is fertile ground for Edgar Reinhard.

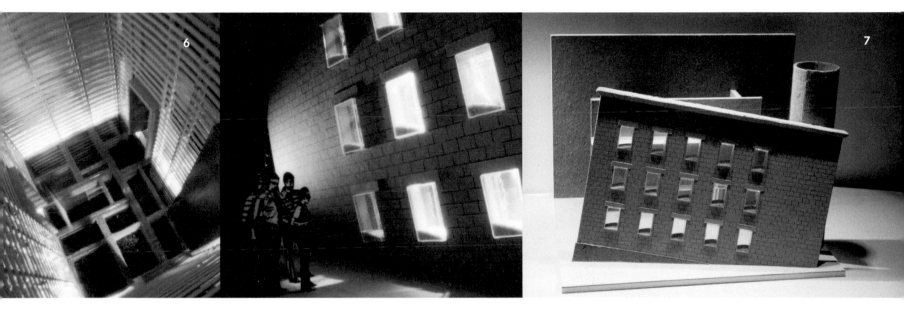

1. Barbara Stöckmann 2. Gerlinde Nelskamp 3. Axel Blieffert 4. Sylvia Becker, Dirk Lützen 5. Christian Richter, Stefan Seidenfaden
6. Katrin Rojahn 7. Kristina Rabbeau, Andrea Höwekenmeier

8. Monika Lassak 9. Cornelia Gerhards, Rainer Goeting 10. Ronald Homringhaus, Heinz Hölters

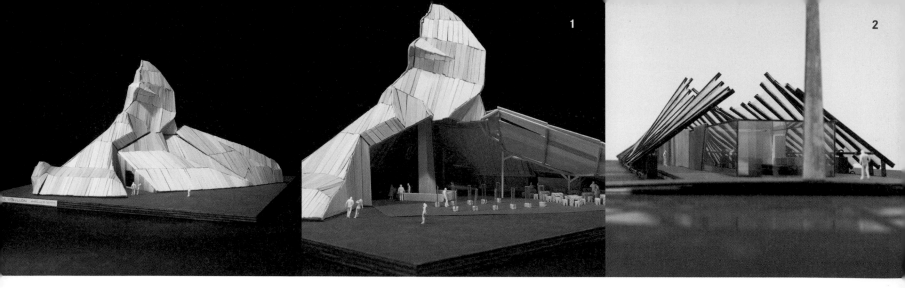

Switzerland was the guest country at the 1998 Frankfurt Book Fair.

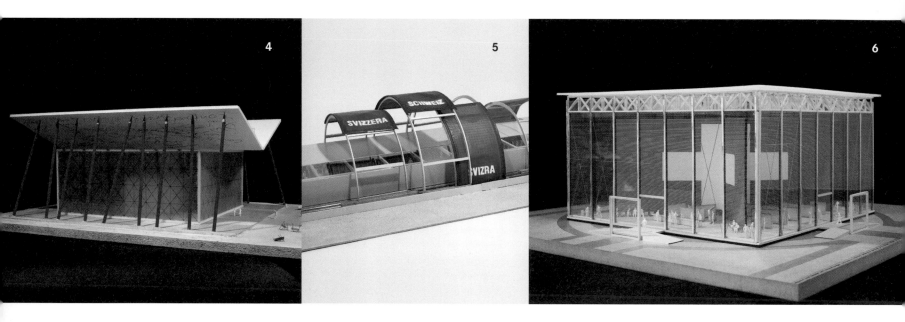

This double page shows students' ideas for a possible approach. Christoph Vitali, who was responsible for the exhibition, decided against an open-air pavilion and commissioned a trade fair hall from Basel architects Diener & Diener.

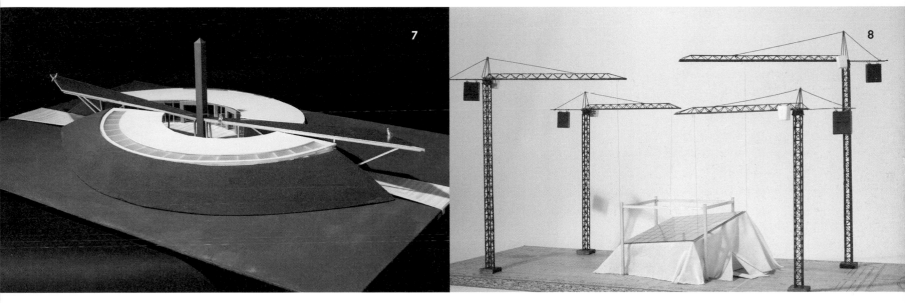

1. Angelica Böhm 2. Kathrin Pösse, Karin Henneke 3. Sabine Müller, Silvia Tirre 4. Ulrich Wagner 5. Silke Sundermeier, Nicole Remmert 6. Ulrike Lenger
7. Mauricia von Eckhardstein, Christina Jerosch 8. Christoph Ziemann

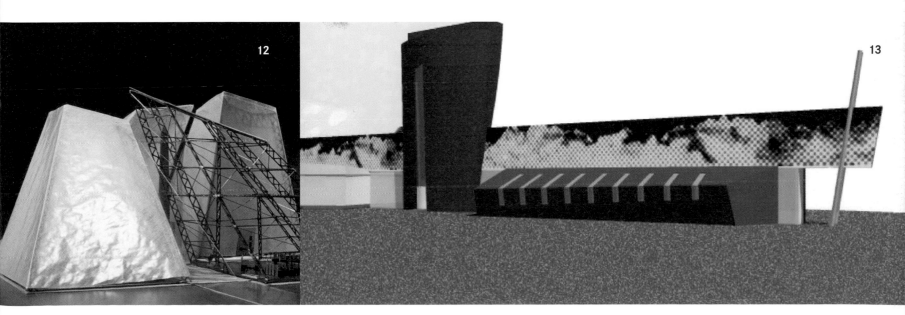

9. Wolfgang Vogler, Stefan Hofmann, Barbara Götsch, Regina Lewandowski 10. Andrea Becker 11. Wilhelm Brentrup, Bernd Caffier, Andrea Tüpper
12. Swantje Kaben 13. Thorsten Stapel

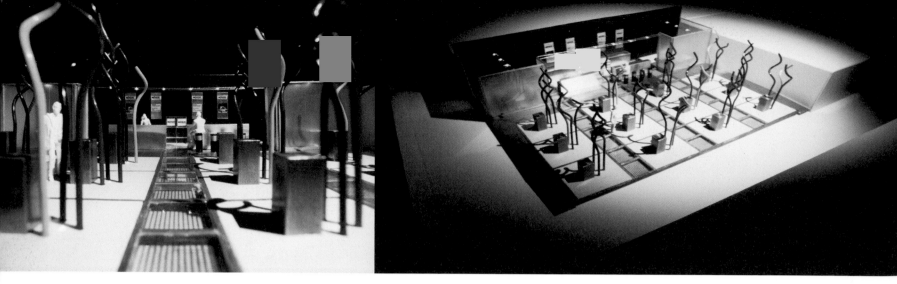

Stand for Wago Verbindungstechnik, a manufacturer of contact elements for electrical circuits. A diploma project by Katrin Neelson.

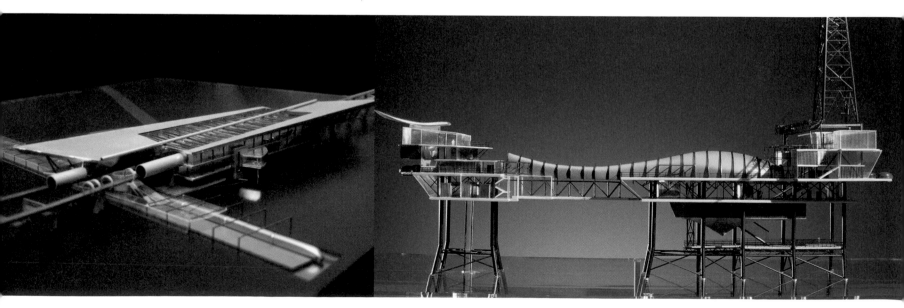

Station for the Berlin – Hamburg magnet train Schwerin.
A diploma project by Michael Heming.

Museum of Oceanography. Conversion of a North Sea oil platform.
A diploma project by Gabi Müller.

1

Some of Reinhard's students were very highly placed in a competition for Mannesmann Röhrenwerke.

1. Dirk Bachmann, Frank Horlitz 2. Yasmin Al Kadri 3. Michael Heming, Ralf Meyer

Exhibition stand for a loudspeaker manufacturer at the radio and television exhibition in Berlin. A diploma project by Yasmin Al Kadri.

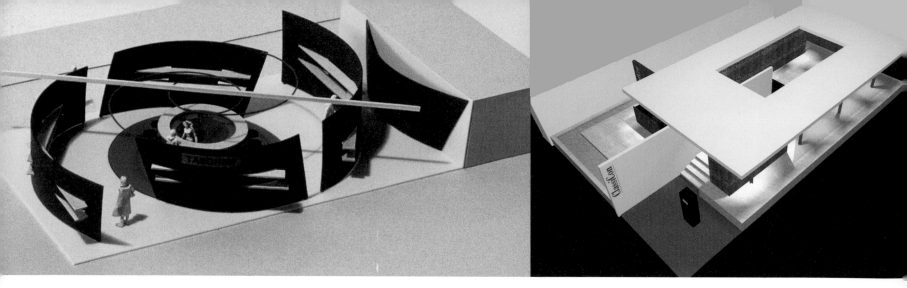

Exhibition stand for Taschen Verlag for the Frankfurt Book Fair. A diploma project by Christina Neher.

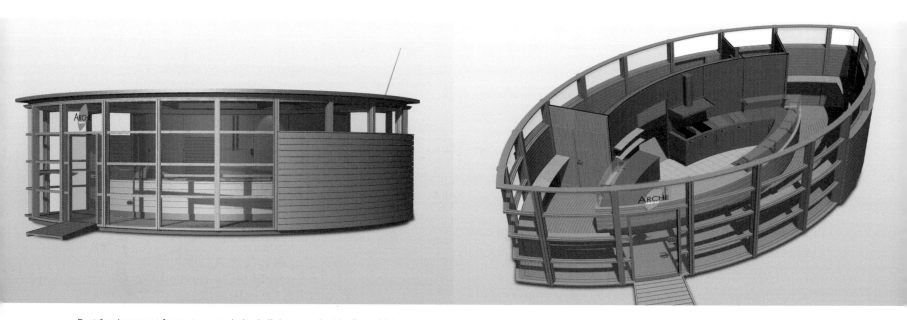

Fast food concept for restaurant chain. A diploma project by Peter Meier.

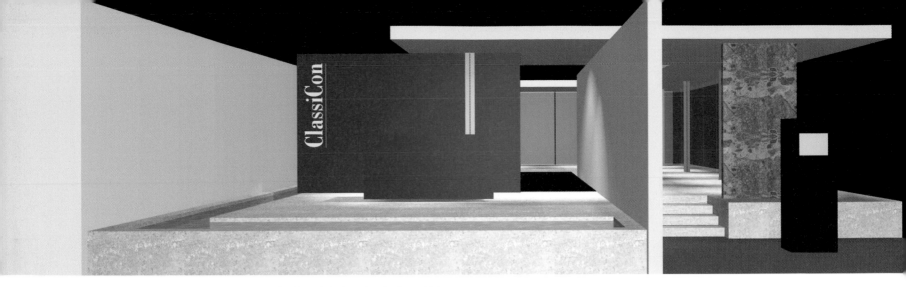

Exhibition stand for Classicon at the Cologne Furniture Fair. A project by Peter Meier.

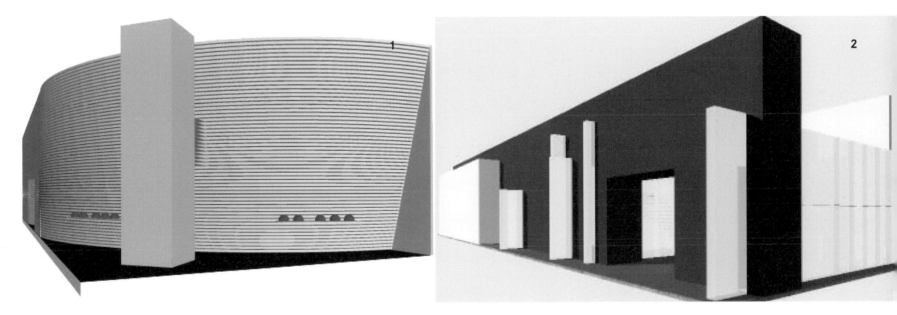

Exhibition stand for IWC, the International Watch Company. Basel Watch and Jewellery Fair.
1. Jens Wehmeier 2. Sabine Dullweber 3. Bettina Brüggemann

Exhibition stand for A. Lange & Söhne, watchmakers. A diploma project by Simone Korte.

Acknowledgements

Edgar Reinhard would like to extend his appreciation and
thanks to all the individuals and companies who have
contributed so much to the projects represented in this book.

Andreoli AG, coating, Volketswil
Blackbox AG, AV, film production, Zurich
Bandi AG, joiner, Oberwil
Badel, electrical contractor, Geneva
C + E, computer engineering, Zurich
Condor Film, AV production, Zurich
Densa AG, packaging, Basel
Egolf AG, packaging, Zurich
Eisenring AG, metal contractor, Jonschwil
Eichenberger Electric AG, theatre lighting, Zurich
Fiberoptic AG, Dietikon,
Fürst, stand contractor, Pratteln
Ferrum AG, foundry, Schafisheim
Galvanic AG, Wädenswil
Gebex AG, plastic processing, Uster
Geyer, air conditioning, Pfäffikon
Gläser AG, joiner, Dättwil
Image Tronic, Newberg, Oregon
Profil Press AG, metalwork, Muri
Protecnic, plastic technology, Adliswil
Primair AG, air conditioning, Herzogenbuchsee
Schneider, steel and metal contractor, Jona
Schefer, steel and metal contractor, Hinwil
Sennhauser, joiner, Feldmeilen
Sound and Light Image AG, theatre lighting, Wetzikon
Sika AG, floor covering, Zurich
Schmidlin, steel and metal contractor, Aesch
Schärrer, lighting, Zurich
Tecnofol AG, plastic processing, Herisau
Texlon AG Giswil, transparent roof systems, Giswil
Temperit AG, safety glass, Hinwil
Technoresin AG, polyester processing, Sihlbrugg
Wespe AG, transport Wetzikon
Wicker Bürki AG, TV aerials, Zurich
Wegmüller AG, packaging transport, Attikon

Frank Baumann, creative director, Zurich
Prof. Reinhart Butter, Ohio State University, Columbus
Prof. Georg Burden, product designer, illustrator, Stuttgart
Dirk Bachmann, assistant, Detmold, Germany
Edy Brunner, designer, Wädenswil
Florin Baeriswyl, architect, Zurich
Carsten Croes, assistant, Muhlheim, Germany
Albert Cinelli, stone sculptor, Wetzikon
Enrico Caspari, set painter, Zuberwangen
Jürg Furrer, illustrator, Seon
Jan Froelich, designer, model building, Zurich
Jacqueline Friederichs, advertising consultant, Zurich
Urs Gerster, architect ETH, Basel
Bernd Grundmann, photographer, Zurich
Urs Greutmann, architect, product designer, Zurich
Peter Hofer, lawyer, Zurich
Marc Hendricks, building contractor, Geneva
Hans Peter Held, writer, Frick
Claudia Imgrüth, advertising consultant, Zurich
Achim Krug, photographer, Mönchengladbach, Germany
Felix Kreyenbühl, advertising consultant, Zurich
Prof. Dr. Andreas Kleinefenn, Detmold, Germany
Prof. Haig Khachatoorian, North Carolina State University, Raleigh
Ivo Kutan, photographer, Zurich
Simone Korte, Dipl. Ing., interior space design, Zurich Gockhausen
Bruno Lienhard, photographer, Zurich
Daniel Lori, product designer, San Francisco, Zurich
Johann May, AV creative director, Newberg, Oregon, USA
Glois Ming, engineer, technical consultant
Prof. Peter Megert, visual consultant, Columbus, Ohio, USA
Peter Osterwalder, static engineer ETH, Oberneunforn
Käti Robert-Durrer, graphic designer, Zurich
Florian Reinhard, student, Zurich Gockhausen
Brigitte Reinhard-Czaja, Zurich Gockhausen
Willi Rieser, artist, illustrator, Augwil

Roger Schmidt, photographer, Zurich
Walter Schefer, engineer, technical consultant, Hinwil
Catherine Schelbert, editor, Bettwil
Jürg Schmid, director of communication IBM, Zurich
Fritz Schoellhorn, product designer, architect, Zurich
Otto Summermatter, trust company, Zurich
Ralph Schraivogel, graphic designer, Zurich
Bruno Spörri, electronic music composer, Oetwil am See
Thorsten Stapel, Dipl. Ing., interior space design, Detmold, Germany
Bertrand Theubet, director Swiss TV, Geneva
Christof Wüthrich, interior space design, Zurich
John Winistoerfer, AV director, producer, Zurich
Prof. Charles Wallschlaeger, Ohio State University, Columbus
Bruno Zemp, portfolio manager, Cham

Book concept:	Adalbert Locher, Edgar Reinhard, Jean Robert
Book design:	Robert & Durrer, Jean Robert, Zurich
Text:	Adalbert Locher
Translation:	Michael Robinson, London
Editing:	David Gibbs, London
German editing:	Simone Korte, Zurich Gockhausen
Editorial consultant:	Stefan Zwicky, architect, designer, Zurich
Photocredits:	Peter Schmid, Architecture without Architects, plate 142, London, 1964, page 22
	Seymour Rosen, Architecture without Architects, plate 126, London, 1964, page 66
	Collection Facetti, Identity Kits: A Pictorial Survey of Visual Signals, page 21, London, 1971, page 160
	Gavin Maxwell, Best of Photojournalism 9, cover Philadelphia, 1984, page 198
	Paul Miller, In Celebration of Ourselves, page 51 San Francisco, 1979, page 254
	Manuel Bauer, pages 298, 300, 302
Digital imaging:	Bildvision, Roger Schmidt, Zurich
Lithography:	Von Känel AG, Zurich
DTP:	Heidy Schuppisser, Baden
Printing:	Fotorotar AG, Egg
Bookbinding:	Burkhardt AG, Mönchaltorf

Printed in Switzerland

Lars Müller Publishers
5401 Baden, Switzerland

ISBN 3-907044-44-4